Fifty

modern bungalows

EDITED BY FELIX WALTER, F. R. I. B. A.

THE ARCHITECTURAL PRESS : LONDON

Printed in Great Britain by Staples Printers Limited, Rochester, Kent, on paper
supplied by Spalding and Hodge, London, and first published in 1955

CONTENTS

4

INTRODUCTION

AFTER NEARLY A DECADE of building restrictions, licensing controls upon all types of house construction were finally abandoned in the Autumn of 1954. As a result, an enormous increase in free-lance building is already noticeable and, during last year alone, private builders were responsible for more than 90,000 new houses for sale—a figure not far short of double the number for the previous year.

Of the two million permanent homes provided since 1945, the great majority were built by local authorities for the purpose of letting to families on the Councils' waiting lists. Although hundreds of thousands have found themselves in new homes, the majority of prospective owners of new houses have been obliged to wait patiently for the fulfilment of their own dreams; but at last these are within reach. It is hoped that this book, which is primarily for the layman, will give him some idea of the many different approaches to house design as well as assist him onto the road towards building his own home.

Amongst the vast numbers of houses springing up everywhere are a profusion of bungalows—a type of building which is not truly indigenous to this country. For its origin one has to look to India where the Empire builders of another age housed themselves in *banglas* or *bungalas*, later modified by the European into the word we all know so well. The bungalow's pedigree was tinged with a degree of romanticism, set as it was in a distant land where comforts were ample, domestic staff readily available and buildings planned in a spacious manner to meet the rigorous climate. How is it then that this single-storey house maintains its perennial popularity in this country?

The answer to this question lies in the special advantages that it has over the two-storey dwelling. From the practical point of view the economics of building are certainly in its favour. Having only the roof to support, foundations and walls need be less massive; the floor can be simply constructed; chimney stacks can be less in height and bulk; plumbing work, if reasonably concentrated, can involve shorter runs of drains and pipework; the omission of the staircase can eliminate not only its cost but the space it would normally occupy. Yet, although financial considerations are important, perhaps the bungalow-owner really prefers this type of house because it is easier to run. The lack of a staircase saves a certain amount of cleaning as well as the physical effort needed to reach the bedrooms and bathroom. Parents are free from the worry of accidents to their children on the stairs, and the aged and infirm prefer to live on one floor. From the aesthetic point of view, also, the bungalow appears less obtrusive than its counterpart and is more easily related to the land on which it rests.

But, with all these and many more advantages, it is disheartening to find the majority of post-war bungalows following the all too familiar pattern dictated by the speculative builder. It is scarcely surprising that these little square boxes have attracted the stigma they deserve. Drive through the outskirts of almost any town and there you will find numbers of these unimaginatively built erections standing on minute plots of land. These 'Chez Nous' and 'Mon Repos' now litter the countryside as though scattered haphazardly from some giant pepper pot.

There is really no reason why a bungalow, however small, should not be a first class piece of architecture, and it is the purpose of this book to illustrate how these single-storey houses can be intelligently planned, soundly constructed to minimize the recurrent expense of maintenance, cheap to run and a joy to live in. And today, there is every justification for taking the fullest advantage of new building techniques, contemporary ideas on planning and design, and the recent advances in materials, equipment and heating.

To take, for example, the item last mentioned—heating. Hitherto the tradition has been to design a bungalow which contains a series of small rooms each in themselves comparatively cheap to heat; but, should the attempt be made to maintain a comfortable temperature throughout the house by means of individual fires lighted in every room, the fuel bill would be prohibitive. Current trends in planning, however, are based upon the principles that the greatest floor space should be given to the rooms most used, and that the layout of the house should be sufficiently flexible to provide space for a multiplicity of uses. This automatically suggests that large areas are more adaptable than small rigid cubicles. Furthermore, a far greater sense of space can be achieved within the area of a small house by this means. But, for any sense of comfort and warmth to be maintained in a large room, the single open fireplace is quite inadequate. It is necessary to provide some supplementary means of heating, as well as to insulate walls, floors, ceilings and windows with greater efficiency to minimize the loss of heat. Described in the *Appendix* at the end of this book are several alternative methods of space or central heating, all of which are based on the same principle—that of sub-floor heating. Instead of radiators standing in the room, the floor itself is warmed at a low temperature to act much as the old radiator but with far greater effect.

In the past, insufficient thought has been given to this problem; but it can no longer be ignored. Indeed, efficient modern heating methods are now revolutionizing our planning conceptions. They make it possible to open up circulation areas otherwise rarely used in cold weather. No longer is it necessary to huddle round the only warm spot in the house —the sitting room fire. And it is not only the space arrangements that are affected. Flooring materials previously considered unsuitable in some rooms can again be used, whilst large window-areas of glass, preferably double-glazed for better insulation, can bring sunlight and warmth into the house, can increase the views from within and, as it were, can reduce the physical barrier between house and garden.

The imaginative use of building materials adds a further interest to the design of the small house today. In an attempt to replace the monotony of traditional brick or plastered walls and tiled roofs, architects are employing new techniques such as the combination of two or more materials of contrasting texture and colour. Local materials, too, are not ignored, for they add interest to a building and are always in harmony with the general character of the district where they are found. The construction and finishes of roofs offer endless variations to the shape of the plan, which is no longer restricted by the limitations imposed upon it by the pitched roof—however sound, basically, that form of construction may be.

It is clear, then, that an infinite number of alternative plan arrangements and uses of materials are available to the owner of a small house—provided it is a 'made-to-measure' one. For, as with clothes so with houses. One has to pay a little more than for the standard speculative building 'off the peg', but one has individual attention, and, in the end, one experiences the satisfaction of owning something of lasting good value. A house specially designed around a family satisfies that family's personal needs, and it simplifies and improves the daily routine of life. It can be designed, for instance, with windows that take in particular views; it can be related to unusal features of the land; the accommodation, fittings and finishes can be planned to suit the owner's preferences and pocket. The whole operation, in fact, can be a fascinating game to obtain the maximum required within the minimum of the finances available.

To the layman, all this may sound most intriguing; but how, he may ask himself, is he to set about the operation in the first place? He may feel sure that he knows what he likes, and believe that he knows what he wants, but, with his restricted experience in the field, he must find someone to translate his needs into the finished article. To whom then should he look for this help? The answer is to be found in the qualified architect, with his many years of professional training and his up-to-date technical knowledge. The houses illustrated in this book are all designed by architects. Furthermore, the great variety of their plan arrangement, of their internal and external treatment and of their cost, suggest that there are endless alternative solutions to what is, after all, basically the same planning problem. The more reason, therefore, why this should be the province only of the trained expert.

This variation in design between one house and another—this individualism—leads to the next important question facing the prospective owner. Which type of design and, therefore, which particular architect will suit his needs? The answer depends largely on the strength of his own convictions. If he can decide that he favours the work he has seen of one particular architect, then a letter directly to him will be the solution. Or if he is fortunate enough to know the owner of the house he admires, a simple introduction to the architect will set the wheels in motion. This contact by recommendation is, in fact, the normal way in which the professional man develops his practice, and, from the layman's viewpoint, it is equally satisfactory since he can discover the architect's characteristics and preferences before approaching him.

But, where neither of these cases apply, the search must follow different lines. By glancing through the technical journals, or the books on the subject, he may discover the type of house he wants, and a note to the Secretary of the R.I.B.A.* will provide him with the architect's address. Alternatively, he can obtain from the same source the address of the Honorary Secretary of the local Allied Society (attached to the R.I.B.A.) that operates in the area where the house is to be built. The Honorary Secretary will supply the names of architects whose practices include house design and, better still, if some explanation is given of the type of house that is wanted, he will recommend one particular architect for the work.

An extremely brief résumé of the architect's duties will be of interest at this point; but for more detailed information a booklet† can be obtained (again from the R.I.B.A.) which explains the scope of the architect's work and his charges, which are controlled by the Institute. In the first place, if the layman is to obtain the greatest assistance from his architect the sooner he appoints him the better, for all manner of queries can arise even when negotiations for the building site are in progress. There may be restrictions on the development of the land, a tree preservation order that controls the felling of timber, an awkward building line, complications regarding access or services to the land, and so on; and in all these matters the architect's experience will be invaluable.

When the site problems have been settled the architect would discuss and list the accommodation, services, fittings and finishes required by the client; and on this basis he would prepare sketch designs and preliminary rough estimates. After modifications or adjustments have been agreed and the preliminary estimate of cost has been accepted by his client, the architect then goes ahead with the preparation of working drawings and specifications which are sent out to several builders who will submit estimates for building the house. Once a tender has been accepted, the client is to all intents and purposes relieved of further responsibility, for his architect prepares the contract between client and builder, provides the builder with all drawings and details, supervises the work itself, certifies payments to the builder and settles the final account.

The architect's fees for these services varies with the cost of the work involved, but the

---

* The Royal Institute of British Architects, 66 Portland Place, London, W.1 (Telephone number: Langham 5721).
† "Conditions of Engagement & Scale of Professional Charges". (Price 6d.)

percentage charge is clearly laid down by the R.I.B.A. There is, in fact, a sliding scale which ranges from 10 per cent for work costing up to £200, to 6 per cent for work costing £4,000 or more. Travelling, out-of-pocket expenses and site survey charges are additional.

A few words about the builder himself may help the layman to appreciate the builder's problems and his attitude towards the job. Careful selection of firms to tender for the work will result in more competitive estimates and, to this end, it is important that all those invited to tender should be of comparable standing one with another and equally acceptable to both client and architect. Thus, unless there is something radically wrong with any of the estimates, the lowest should be accepted on principle. It is equally important, once the contract has been signed, that there should be the minimum of interference or alteration on the job. Variations and delays are extremely expensive, for they tend to upset the builder's site organization and, on a comparatively small job such as a house perhaps in an isolated area, the economic planning and sequence of trades is, to say the least, complicated. It is, then, in the interests of both client and builder, not to mention the architect, that nothing should be left to chance. The architect must assure himself that his client is fully aware of all aspects of the design and, in this way, most of those tiresome second thoughts will be avoided.

All this points to one conclusion. The same efficiency and care that has been applied at the planning and design stages must be continued throughout the subsequent building operations. In fact, the only way to lower maintenance costs in the years to follow is by careful detailing and thorough site supervision by a competent qualified architect. A well planned and soundly constructed house will retain its value long after the speculative-built one has divulged all its weaknesses; and, in the event of selling the property, the well-built house will always attract a much higher price on the open market.

Finally, if any one stage in the creation of a bungalow is more important than another for the layman-client, it is surely the formulation of precise requirements right at the beginning. It is, in fact, impossible to over-estimate the value of a clear-cut, well considered programme, which is neither over ambitious nor excessively modest; but it is difficult, if not impossible, for the layman to know how much floor space, fittings and equipment and standards of finish his limited capital will purchase. However, if he can decide what he wants regardless of size, quantity or quality, his architect will advise him on the cost. To this end, the following brief notes may assist those immersed in the preliminary stages, and serve to remind them of the odds and ends as well as the more obvious needs. In no way does this check list claim to be exhaustive, but it does cover the majority of items normally encountered in the average house. What is omitted from his house, and what is included, will be dictated by the layman's own preferences and, of course, by his purse. How the jig-saw puzzle of his final needs is put together will depend upon a hundred and one influences, but, above all, it will depend upon the skill of his architect in fitting the pieces into place.

A CHECK-LIST OF NEEDS AND SOME PLANNING SUGGESTIONS

The site and landscaping

Seclusion is a joy, but avoid buying more land than you can afford to maintain. Gardens planned carefully with flowering trees and shrubs and with limited areas of cultivation are less likely to transform the enthusiastic house-owner into an exhausted slave of the garden. Make the best use of sloping land to add interest to the house and garden layout. Sloping sites are not necessarily more expensive to build upon than flat areas; it all depends upon how they are handled.

When siting the house itself, be sure that every advantage is taken of existing cover, trees, shrubs, falls and views. Protect yourself both from prevailing cold winds and nearby eyesores belonging to your neighbours!

Orientation, or relationship with compass-bearings, is very important. The best site falls to the south-west or south with the road on the northern boundary; land sloping upwards to the south with the view to the north is difficult to handle. The finest view is so frequently on the wrong side of the house, perhaps to the north-west or north-east, but skilful planning may 'bring' these views within reach, through a picture-window or some other feature.

Avoid the impression that your house has been placed on the site without regard to the development of the land around it; a building line may have dictated the minimum distance of the house from the road, but that is all. The layout of the site should be considered as part of the planning of the house; means should be found to suggest that one is part of the other.

Shapes

Architecture is a pliant art and, so long as the construction is not unduly complicated, there is no reason why some amusement should not be introduced into the general design; for houses are created for occupation by human beings and not by machines. Irregular shapes skilfully handled, although unconventional, can be an immense relief from the rigidity of the square or rectangle, but there should be sound reason for them.

The house and its cells

Sixty years ago it was normal for many houses to contain a drawing room, dining room, breakfast room or morning room, the master's study, billiards room, sewing room, flower room, and so on.

But, for reasons discussed already, the contemporary house has to be compactly designed and the floor space used for more than one purpose. Thus one has to decide what operations are to be combined within the same areas, so that these multi-purpose rooms may be suitably planned and equipped. No single small house of today would include all the cells enumerated below, but the list attempts to cover all those rooms and spaces from which the contemporary house is designed.

The *fittings* for each room, printed in italics and marked (F), are noted first, and the *planning suggestions*, marked (P), follow:

ENTRANCE HALL

(F) *Hanging cupboard, mat-sinking, separate letter-box away from front door, a place for umbrellas.*

(P) Provide enough space to open the door to visitors without feeling cramped. In the interests of privacy, avoid passing the living and bedroom windows to reach the front door. The open hall with two fully glazed walls is attractive but offers no protection against the unwelcome visitor, including, in rural areas, the possible formal call upon the new resident by other inhabitants for friendly or inquisitive purposes.

CLOAKROOM

(F) *Hanging cupboards, shelving, lavatory basin and splash back, w.c. (perhaps separated from cloak room), hooks, boot cupboard, towel rail, toilet paper holder, mirror.*

(P) Direct access from the outside is an advantage, for it can then act as a 'dirty' entrance as well.

FLOWER ROOM

(F) *Sink, draining board, working table top, vase cupboards and shelves, soap container, towel rail.*

(P) If required at all, this could be combined with the cloakroom. Protect the walls behind the sink and drainer with tiles, etc.

CORRIDORS AND LOBBIES

Avoid them as far as possible for they are wasteful, costly and need cleaning. L-shaped corridors are particularly unpleasant for they instil the sense of enclosure and suggest muddled planning. Where corridors are inevitable, consider widening where most used and reducing the width where there is least traffic; the tapering effect can add interest to the plan but complicates the laying of close-carpeting. Lobbies between the kitchen and dining or living rooms are unnecessary if the doors are properly fitted and the kitchen is efficiently ventilated. Small lobbies about one yard square with doors in adjoining walls are tiresome to negotiate with a tea trolley; angles of doors and frames get chipped and damaged.

LIVING ROOM

(F) *Bookshelves cupboards, heated window for plants, aquarium tank, built-in radio, and/or T.V. sets, open fireplace, generous hearth, log cupboard, shelves for* objets d'art.

(P) This area is the most used in the house and should be as large as possible. Avoid doors near the radius of the sitting space around the fireplace and restrict exits into the garden to the opposite end of the room. A pipe under the floor from the outside to near the fireplace grate will reduce draughts in the room. Very large windows should be double glazed to improve the thermal insulation. As an extremely broad generalization, the best orientation is south-south-east, but each case has to be determined on its own merits, for many other considerations have to be taken into account as well. Limit the rigid barriers between the living area and the garden; the omission of conventional window sills, with glazing running down to the floor, or to very low sills, will help to achieve this. By combining the living and dining rooms a greater sense of space can be obtained; the dining area could be recessed off the living area to simplify curtaining or closing-off at times.

DINING ROOM

(F) *Service hatch, two-way cupboards to kitchen, wine cupboard, sideboard for carving, etc.*

(P) Orientate so that the early morning as well as the mid-day sun penetrates the room; an excess of sun or glare, both of which are infrequent, can always be controlled by Venetian blinds which add to the decorative appearance of the room. Limit the floor space by assessing the maximum number of persons likely to dine at one time. Consider having an access from the dining room directly onto a paved terrace, well protected from the winds, for meals outside; this might take the form of a loggia, patio or pergola covered area. The dining room may have to be a multi-purpose room. Decide where the sewing machine is to be used, for instance, where school homework is to be done, where Father writes in peace if he hasn't a study, and so on. Extend the window treatment of the dining area in a similar manner to that in the general living area; do not be afraid of large windows so long as the space-heating is adequate.

KITCHEN

(F) *Service hatch with two-way cupboards and drawers for storage of china, glass, cutlery, condiments and the like. Access from dining room. Cupboards for dry goods, cooking equipment, trays; a warmed cupboard for drying tea cloths. Racks for pots, pans and their lids. Space for the cooker, sink and draining boards, roller towel fitting and tea-cloth rails, washing machine, refrigerator, refuse bin and ironing board. Long term storage cupboards for the fruit bottling sterilizer, preserving pan, empty jars and bottles, etc.*

(P) Kitchen planning is a personal problem and generalizations are misleading. Some prefer windows facing north, others east, or south-east; some prefer a small working kitchen, others a larger space to take a preparation table in the middle; and again there is the combination of the kitchen-dining room or the compromise with a bar-fitting between the dining room and kitchen for casual meals. The immense variety of alternative layouts, as well as fittings and equipment, have made kitchen planning a complicated business, but it should never be forgotten that a room is more cheerful where the sun can penetrate and where a pleasant view into the garden exists. The kitchen needs heating as much as the living area; many heat storage and other types of cookers emit insufficient warmth into the room.

LARDER

(F) *Shelving, cold slab of marble, slate or tiles, vegetable racks, egg racks, ceiling hooks for hanging game, etc., deep freeze cabinet.*

(P) The average house, even with a refrigerator, needs a larder big enough to enter; the cupboard ventilated with a couple of air bricks is not good enough in a new house. The window should be fitted with a flyscreen and there should be adequate narrow shelving closely spaced for storage of bottled fruit and jam, as well as wider shelving for day to day use. Where capital outlay permits, consider the installation of a heat pump unit which, by extracting heat from the air in the larder, reduces the temperature therein and, at the same time, provides domestic hot water at a very modest cost (see *Appendix*, page 112).

BROOM CUPBOARD

For no good reason, the cupboard for brushes and brooms is located too often in the kitchen; it is better placed in a more central position between the bedroom and living areas to avoid unnecessary traffic into the kitchen. There should be sufficient space for brushes, brooms, dust pan, electric polisher and vacuum cleaner, dusters, polishing and scrubbing materials. A benefit, perhaps, would be the inclusion of a small drip or slop-sink for emptying buckets of dirty water, etc., with hot and cold water taps above. A space of about ten square feet would be adequate for everything. Rails for hanging floor cloths to dry are useful, as is plenty of natural ventilation.

BEDROOM

(F) *Built-in wardrobe fitted for hanging clothes (minimum net depth: 1 foot, 9 inches), trays for smaller articles, shoe racks, etc., dressing table (possibly for use as a writing desk as well), bookshelves, bedside cabinets for oddments, lavatory basin with a generous splashback, towel rail and mirrors.*

(P) A good orientation is south-east. West is too hot in summer and north is cold and cheerless. Low window sills, or none at all, give wider views into the garden; french doors onto a paved terrace add to the interest of the room and are a joy during summer months; it would be foolish to include these if the orientation is north-west or north. For ease in making beds, only the heads should be against the wall; this may be difficult if not impossible to achieve in the small single bedroom. Rooms should be designed so that the bed can be placed in more than one position to allow for a variation of arrangement; some knowledge of how the room will be furnished later is essential for flexibility. For children, rooms might be designed as study-bedrooms where they may find peace and quiet; but some method of heating would have to be provided. For young children, space can be saved by the use of two-tier bunks, one of which could be removed as the children grow up. Finally, avoid bedroom doors opening onto the entrance hall; single-storey houses can and should offer complete seclusion for sleeping and bathing facilities.

DRESSING ROOM

Space rarely permits this, but a dressing room can be justified if used also as a spare single bedroom, or even as a study.

BATHROOM

(F) *Bath, lavatory basin, w.c., bidet, shower, hand sprays, medicine cabinet, built-in soap recess for bath, glass shelving, heated towel rail, toilet paper container, mirror.*

(P) The bathroom should be nearest to the main bedroom and, as in the case of the latter, should not open onto the entrance hall. If one w.c. only is to be provided, this should be in a separate compartment. For the early morning sun, the bathroom should face south-east or east. Flooring should be warm under foot and one of the best materials for this purpose is cork; if sub-floor space-heating is provided the choice of floor finish is very much greater.

WATER-CLOSET

Another compartment which should never open directly onto the entrance hall; privacy and acoustics should be studied and some background heating provided. This is one of the few places where a small lobby three feet square is really justified. A small lavatory basin and towel rail should be included wherever a w.c. is planned.*

LINEN AND AIRING CUPBOARDS

These should not be planned within kitchens and bathrooms because of steam and occasional inaccessibility. Linen should not be stored for any length of time in high temperature airing cupboards as heat will ultimately destroy linen fibres. Two compartments are preferable therefore; one dry cupboard for storage and another warmed for airing.

CUPBOARDS AND STORAGE

Where the initial capital outlay prohibits built-in fittings, plan so that they may be added later if required. Hanging cupboards for clothes are good sound baffles between one room and another; by careful arrangement, cupboards in adjourning rooms can be 'staggered' so that the whole wall is a series of cupboards facing opposite directions; this is tidy in appearance. Avoid noisy cupboard door catches and running tracks to side-hung and sliding doors. To simplify cleaning, keep the bottom cupboard shelf in line with the top of the skirting board running round the walls.

Storage space is needed for spare blankets, pillows and even the odd mattress, not to mention a host of other household goods which are better put away than left about to collect dust.

BOX AND TRUNK ROOM

The contemporary house often has no roof space, and even cold water cisterns have to be worked in with some ingenuity; thus the large storage space of old, which accommodated a jumble of discarded chattels, is less in evidence today. Trunks and suitcases still need a home; even a space three or four feet square might suffice. Other alternatives are some extra deep cupboards at high level which are difficult to reach

---

* For a study in discretion, do not overlook the small classic, entitled *The Specialist*, which, though an essay on the w.c.'s forebears, includes imaginative alternatives for the evasion of embarrassment.

for normal day to day use, or racks at high level in the garage; but wherever the storage, it must be absolutely dry.

MISCELLANEOUS

The foregoing notes cover the basic accommodation within the average house, but there are naturally many other interests and personal possessions for which individual clients would want to find space, and a random selection of these is as follows:

Boiler room. Flue for boiler (fuel store adjoining). For greatest efficiency, the floor should be lower than the normal house floor.

Children's study or playroom. Cupboards and bookshelves, wash basin or sink and drainer with hot and cold water, blackboard.

Darkroom (photographic). Sinks and drainers, working top, cupboards, hot and cold water supply, light lock, ventilation.

'Dirty' entrance from the garden. Possibly combined with the cloakroom, with shoe cleaning facilities.

Drying room. Located next to boiler room for clothes drying, etc.

Pram store. With under cover access to house, lockable and dry.

Sewing room. Large cutting-out table, hinged full-length mirrors.

Study. Writing desk, cupboards and shelves.

Wine cellar. Sadly too often omitted in this misguided age.

Workshop. Should be absolutely dry, with heating available. For hobbies, carpentry, etc.; and probably containing bench, shelving, tool cupboards or drawers, gas point for heating glue; also space for storing timber and other stock material. Direct access to garage is useful for supplementary working space.

Outbuildings, drives, etc.

General. In planning the new home, the immediate and future development of the site should be considered as well as the house proper, for these are not two separate problems but one. Behind all this comprehensive planning lies the desire for a layout which appears as a related conception complete in itself. Therefore anticipate, as far as can be, all those odd sheds and extensions that tend to destroy the simple unity of a scheme.

Garage. A garage is less costly to build when attached to the house; a further advantage if it is used as a multi-purpose space is its accessibility. In this country the garage should be linked to the house by a covered way. The width of garage should be such that car doors on either side can be opened without hitting the walls; and the length should be sufficient to allow one to crank the car without having to move it first. Double doors at either end can reduce the length of the garage, for end-space is then unnecessary; also the washdown, instead of being visible from the drive, can then be out of sight at the opposite end of garage.

A recess to accommodate work bench, shelving and cupboard for spares is an advantage. Lightly constructed walls and roof faced with fibreboard internally are very much warmer than brickwork or plastered blocks; a garage located near the boiler room can benefit from the surplus radiated heat from the installation, unless the latter is heavily lagged.

In the illustrations of houses which follow it should be noted that the total floor areas include the garage areas where these form part of the design, unless it is otherwise stated.

Drives. The general shape and surface finish of a drive can make or mar the approach to the house. Drive layouts should be fluid in design and planned for the easy use of the car driver; the turning space should be neither mean nor extravagant. A parking space for visitors' cars off the main driveway, if not a necessity, is a great benefit. The layout should allow the car to approach to within a few feet of the front door, which is best protected by some kind of projecting porch or, at least, it should be recessed behind the main wall to offer protection to those awaiting entry during inclement weather. Large expanses of concrete appear crude and unsightly; they should have a top dressing, if concrete is used as a base, unless there is some good reason for omitting it. The type of construction and finish will depend upon the locality of the site and the availability of material but, whatever this may be, the drive should blend with the building materials of the house to avoid harsh discord.

Fuel stores. There are many occasions when fuel stores have to be located in an extension rather than forming part of the main house. For efficiency, stores should adjoin the fires they supply, i.e., boiler fuel next to the boiler, coal and logs nearest to the open fires most used. If this is impossible, handling and carrying should be reduced to a minimum. Access should be by a paved and covered way. Floors of stores should be laid to a fall, and not horizontally, to encourage fuel to gravitate towards the access door or opening. Fuel stores for solid fuel boilers, when the latter are at basement level, can be conveniently planned above them to eliminate the handling of fuel altogether. The flow of fuel should be controlled by a cut-off door similar in action to the chimney damper of an ordinary boiler flue. Artificial light is necessary in all fuel stores for use at night. A hole in the door or, better still, a small 'pilot' lamp in the kitchen will warn when the lights have been left on.

Other buildings. In addition to the foregoing a number of other buildings, more applicable perhaps to the rural house, may need consideration:

Children's play area. This might have a miniature house or a covered space without walls.

Greenhouses. The orientation will depend upon the type of greenhouse to be built. If heating from the central plant is required, the building should be near to the main house, but it is often more economical to have independent heating by oil or electricity if the heating periods are only sporadic.

Henhouse and run. It seems inevitable that the run should be an eyesore; an evergreen hedge will help to conceal it.

Junk room. As a supplement or alternative to the indoor box room.

Machinery and tool store. For the lawn mower, wheelbarrow, cultivator, garden tools, etc.

Pig pens and runs. Although for obvious reasons these are best away from the house, they should be reasonably near to reduce time and effort in carrying feeding materials to and fro.

Potting shed. Shelving, bins, racks, etc.

W.C. (outside). Unless there is a 'dirty' access to the cloakroom, an extra w.c. is an advantage. Finally, the possible need for an *apple and fruit store* and a *bicycle store* should not be overlooked.

A note on building costs

Before concluding, a point must be mentioned concerning the building costs of the houses illustrated in this book. It should be noted that the cost given for each house is the figure that was ruling during the actual year of building. Because of the increased rates of labour and material, building prices have risen from time to time and, in order to compare the original capital outlay with current costs, the paragraphs which follow will be of assistance. To make it quite clear, it would be as well to state also that the cost given in each case does not include the purchase of the land, site development and professional charges unless otherwise stated. And, for those who wish to analyse the plans more closely, the area of a house for estimating purposes is taken within the outside walls and includes all floor space, corridors, lobbies, internal walls, partitions, chimney stacks, etc., within that area.

Taking mid-1945 as a starting point, the following percentage figures (which, it should be noted, are approximate only) will serve as a rough guide to show how building costs of previous years can be compared with those of today.

The amount per cent that costs had risen by mid-1954 is as follows:

Approximately 75 per cent above mid-1945 costs

,,	51 ,,	,,	,,	late-1947 costs
,,	$41\frac{1}{2}$,,	,,	,,	Dec. 1947 costs
,,	$32\frac{3}{4}$,,	,,	,,	mid-1950 costs
,,	29 ,,	,,	,,	early-1951 costs
,,	$1\frac{1}{2}$,,	,,	,,	early-1952 costs

Between 1945 and the first quarter of 1952 costs increased, and they never decreased; fairly progressive rises, therefore, should be visualized in between the key years given above, except late in 1947 and during 1951 when sharp rises took place. The crucial year, as far as this book is concerned, is 1951 when a very rapid rise indeed occurred. Since that year the encouraging sign is that the increases in the rates of labour have been offset by the gradual fall in the cost of materials; building costs have therefore fluctuated only slightly. Thus, for all practical purposes, a house built at the end of 1954, or the beginning of 1955, would cost only a fractional amount more than one built early in 1952.

It should be understood that these percentage increases give a picture of the rise in costs in general as, in calculating them, all types of buildings have been taken into consideration, collectively. With one individual type, such as the small house, there might be some variations from these figures. They will suffice, however, to give a fairly realistic idea of what the houses—those built prior to 1952, in particular—would cost today.* If required, more precise information is obtainable elsewhere.† Finally, one fact provokes some thought, and that is that between the last pre-war year, 1939, and 1946 building costs had doubled, whilst today they have more than trebled.

---

* The costs are included of all the houses illustrated in this book, except in two cases where the costs were not obtainable.

† *The Builder* (Catherine Street, Aldwych, W.C.2), for instance, publishes a useful chart which shows, at a glance, how building costs, the price of materials and wages have fluctuated since 1939.

THE HOUSES ILLUSTRATED *on the pages which follow are arranged, for convenience, according to their cost, beginning with the most expensive houses*

designed by **T. MELLOR**

At top: the house from the south. Above: the living room looking towards the dining space which is down two steps and is screened by a five foot high bookshelf. Right: the front entrance.

ACCOMMODATION WAS REQUIRED for a family of four. A direct relationship between the indoor and outdoor living areas was aimed at, but without using glass walls or an extremely open plan. The site is a clearing in a wood, and over the south boundary wall—about 100 feet from the house—is a road, and then an open space with the Ribble estuary beyond. The house is sited so that the living room obtains this south view, while the projecting bedroom wing hides another house to the south-east. It was built in 1953.

CONSTRUCTION. Brick load-bearing walls. North elevation and gable walls in buff-coloured facing bricks. South elevation, and all sides of south wing, plastered and painted grey-white and grey-green. *Roofs:* pitched roof, tiled; monopitch roof, Stramit panels with bituminous felt finish. *Floors:* suspended timber or solid concrete floors finished with slate slabs in hall and cloakroom and cork tiles in dining room and playroom.

HEATING. Concealed ceiling panels heated by low pressure hot water from Janitor anthracite boiler thermostatically controlled. Living room heating fitted with motorized valve controlled by room thermostat. Open fires in living room and main bedroom.

AREAS. 1,976 sq. ft, excluding garage, but including room above. 2,176 sq. ft including garage.

COST. Approximately £6,000. Approximately 55s. 1d. per sq. ft.

Above: the house from the south-west. Walls are painted either grey-white or grey-green, and woodwork is white. To the west of the living room (see plan below) is a terrace with screen walls and outdoor fireplace. On the north-east side of the house there is an entrance for vehicles from an existing drive which leads from the road on the south.

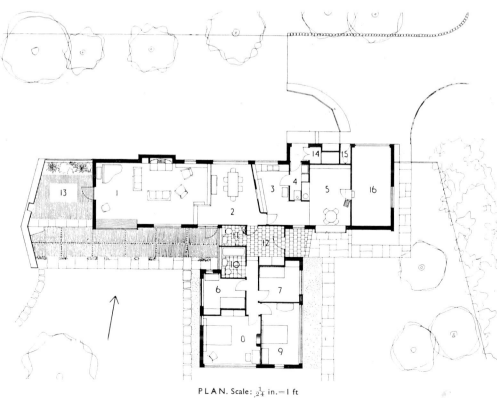

PLAN. Scale: $\frac{1}{24}$ in. = 1 ft

KEY TO
PLAN
 1. Living room.
 2. Dining room.
 3. Kitchen.
 4. Utility.
 5. Playroom.
 6. Bedroom.
 7. Bedroom.
 8. Bedroom.
 9. Bedroom.
10. Bathroom.
11. Cloakroom.
12. Hall.
13. Terrace.
14. Fuel.
15. W.C.
16. Garage
    (Studio over
    with access by
    ladder from
    playroom).

17

designed by **SYDNEY GREENWOOD AND HOWARD N. MICHELL**

Above: the house from the garden, viewed from the south-west. Left: the hall, looking towards the north window. Below: the house, and approach, from the north-west.

THE GROUNDS OF THIS well-equipped house contain many fine trees and an orchard. The house was completed in 1954 and it was planned —with large areas of glazing—to take in the fine views beyond the garden which falls away to the south. The owner required it to be large enough to entertain friends, yet small enough for his wife to run with occasional help.

CONSTRUCTION. 10½ in. cavity walls with 4½ in. facing bricks. *Roof:* 20 degree pitched roof with trusses at 2 ft centres, covered with Canadian cedar shingles. *Floors:* concrete (see *Heating*). *Internal finishes:* Perfonit acoustic tiled ceilings in living/dining room; plasterboard ceilings elsewhere; walls generally plastered and either wallpapered or painted; floors screeded and carpeted, except for hall floor in Nabresina marble. *Thermal insulation:* all windows, except in bathrooms, double-glazed; living/dining room windows glazed with Insulight; Carda windows in bedrooms and study; bituminous fibreglass laid over ceiling joists; 4 in. Thermalite for inner leaf of walls and internal walls.

HEATING. Sub-floor heating with heating coils laid over 2 in. woodwool slabs and covered with 3½ in. concrete, screeded.

AREA. 2,260 sq. ft. including garage and outbuildings; (house alone: 1,735 sq. ft).

The living room with, on the left, the dining space on the upper level, with treads to the steps in Nabresina marble and risers in sycamore onyx. The specially designed piece of furniture at the top of the steps is a combined sideboard and cocktail cabinet. The large sliding windows take in the wide and distant views southwards. It was to make the most of these views, also, that a recessed and sheltered court was planned to the east of the living area (see plan below).

The west wall of the living room. On the right are the steps leading up to the hall which are seen in the centre illustration on the opposite page. The wall around the fireplace is papered, and the built-in fitting next to it contains an aquarium, a radiogram, cupboards and bookshelves. The woods used for the various built-in fitments in the house were rosewood, beech, mahogany and French walnut.

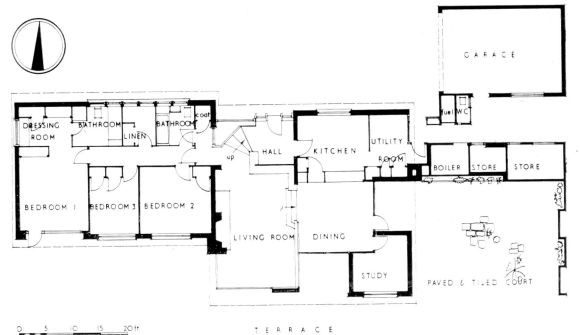

designed by MICHAEL LYELL

DESIGNED BY AN ENGLISH architect for an English owner, this house will be built near the edge of the cliffs half a mile from San Feliu de Guixols. The montage-composition, illustrated above, views the site from the north-west. The beautiful, rugged terrain abounds with rocky outcrops, cacti and cork trees, and there are magnificent views.

CONSTRUCTION. Constructional system of timber trusses at 3 metre centres supported on hardwood columns or load bearing walls. (Layout of house is based on grid unit of 1 metre.) Walls of local stone or Spanish brick, rendered white externally and plastered internally. *Roof:* joist construction spanning between trusses, and Spanish tiles. *Ceilings:* polished vertical boarding or plastered ceilings. *Floors:* concrete sub-floor finished with parquet and terrazzo tiles.

HEATING. Hot water provided by four electric storage heaters. Open fires in living rooms and outside barbecue; electric fires elsewhere. (No central heating as house is only for summer use.)

AREAS. House: approximately 2,230 sq. ft. Outbuildings, including carport: 680 sq. ft.

COST. Estimated at approximately £6,000, excluding built-in furniture and fittings.

A plan-view of the roof of the model.

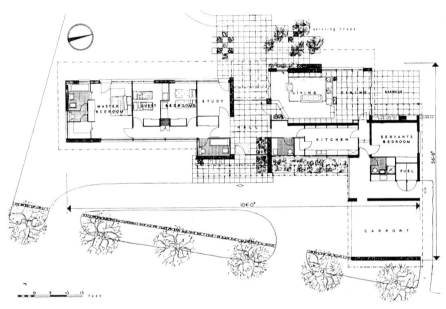

PLAN

Above: a drawing of the house from the south-east. Left: the model, viewed from the north-west. On the west side the roof overhangs six feet to protect rooms from the sun, and external lighting effects will make the roof appear to 'float' at night. Ventilation by adjustable glass louvres allows the air to pass right through the rooms at ceiling level. Main rooms had to face the sea; therefore, to give it interest, the long narrow plan which resulted is broken up with patios and flagstone terraces.

desig ied by **IAN WARWICK**

Above: the house from the east. Below: the hall looking south-east.

THE LONG APPROACH to this house runs south-east from the road on the north. It leads to a Saxon mound (known as Risinghoe Castle) which obscures the views that exist of the river Ouse. By siting the house on the southern slopes of this mound, the architect has contrived to withhold these views to the visitor until the house has actually been entered. But, once inside, a panoramic scene of the winding river is unfolded through the windows.

CONSTRUCTION. Cavity brick walls with inner skin of thermalite blocks. *Roof:* ¾ in. asphalte, 2 in. cork insulation and rafters. *Floors:* partly 4 in. site concrete on hardcore and partly reinforced concrete with patent pre-cast flooring; wood block finishes in main rooms, tiles in bathroom and kitchen. *Windows:* double glazed.

HEATING. Space-heating by oil-fired heater.

AREAS. Ground level: approximately 1,600 sq. ft. Total area approximately 2,124 sq. ft.

COST. £5,500. Cost per sq. ft: 51s. 9d. (Costs are approximate only.)

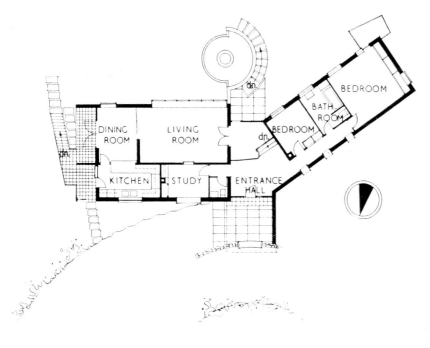

The sloping site — near Castle Mill Farm, Renhold —enabled the east wing to be raised above the ground, thus obtaining a good view. Beneath this wing is a 'promenade' and play space (seen below the balcony in the top illustration on the opposite page). Steps will later be built to lead down from this balcony (see plan). Below: the house, from the south-west, when nearing completion in 1954.

GROUND FLOOR
PLAN. Scale: $\frac{1}{8}$ in. = 1 ft

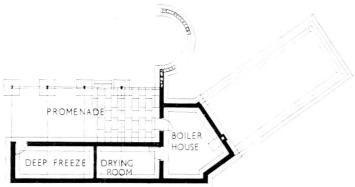

FOUNDATION PLAN

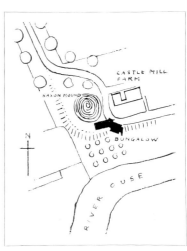

SKETCH OF SITE PLAN

designed by **STILLMAN AND EASTWICK-FIELD** (*assistant architect: Ralph Smorczewski*)

Two drawings of the house by Ralph Smorczewski: (at top) from the north-west, and (above) from the south.

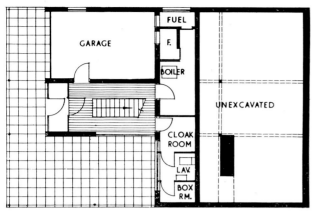

LOWER LEVEL PLAN

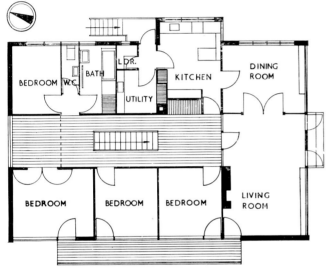

UPPER LEVEL PLAN. Scale: $\frac{1}{16}$ in. = 1 ft

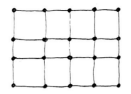

1. *How the architects solved the planning problems (a) to (e), described in the text, is shown here. Firstly, the sloping site and the unstable soil necessitated pile foundations and therefore a frame structure.*

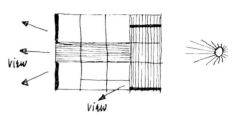

2. *The importance of combining the sun and the view influenced the relationship between the hall and the living room, the hall being conceived as part of the living space.*

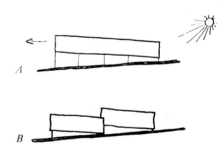

3. *As stated, the client required a balcony to all bedrooms, all bedrooms to be above ground level, and no changes of level for the living and sleeping area. This led to the conception of a house built against the slope (see A) rather than of a house built with the slope (see B).*

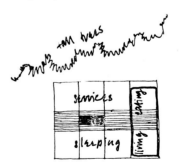

4. *The final conception: a compact and isolated unit in contrast to the surrounding land. The focal point of the house is the staircase, with the surrounding hall which provides a visual link between sun and view, south and north. Around this focal point revolve the four main functions of the house: sleeping, living, eating and service.*

THE SITE, a long, narrow one, slopes north towards the road and has a view over Redhill. There is the possibility of the soil, an unstable sandy clay, sliding. The client required: (a) accommodation for four, plus one guest bedroom; (b) sun and view to the living room and all bedrooms if possible; (c) a balcony to all bedrooms; (d) all bedrooms to be above ground level; (e) no changes of level. How these problems were solved is shown in the right-hand column.

CONSTRUCTION. Reinforced concrete frame up to upper floor level; timber structure above. Timber stud walls at upper level; stone panel walls at lower level. Reinforced concrete raft floor. Timber joist flat roof. Upper level finished externally with weather boarding. Internal finishes: end grip hardwood blocks on floors; plaster painted walls and ceilings; hardwood strings and treads on staircase. Insulight is used in living room and dining room. Floor panel heating is to be installed.

AREAS. Living area: 1,600 sq. ft. Total area, including garage, hall, boiler room etc: approximately 2,000 sq. ft.

GORTNAMONEY, MOIRA, NORTHERN IRELAND

designed by E. W. BEAUMONT (*of* HOUSTON AND BEAUMONT)

Above: the house from the south-west. The chimney in the west wall is built of local stone. On the south side the large sliding windows of the living room and the third bedroom (which is also used as a study) open onto a terrace. The site of two acres is one mile from the village of Moira. A plan of the house is illustrated on page 108, and it shows the layout of the floor panel heating system which has been installed. Below: the front entrance from the north-east.

SITUATED EIGHTEEN MILES from Belfast, this house stands on a site which slopes towards the road on the south. After considerable thought the architects decided not to adopt an open plan, but to keep the various activities separated. The house, therefore, was planned in three zones as follows: (1) the living room and the third bedroom (also used as a study), with both rooms having easy access to two terraces on the south and north sides; (2) the two other bedrooms, to face north, east and south with a bathroom *en suite*; (3) the kitchen and the dining room adjacent to each other. As planned in this way, advantage is taken of a view to the south, the sun terrace in the north-west angle is given privacy, and the kitchen and dining room windows get the morning and evening sun. The plan of this house, which was built in 1952, is illustrated on page 108.

CONSTRUCTION. Traditional concrete foundations. 11 in. cavity walls finished externally with Stonite rendering in white. Internal walls of brick or breeze, finished either with rustic bricks or with plaster. *Roof:* timber roof covered with cedar shingles. *Floors:* concrete floors, insulated with vermiculite concrete, and finished with granolithic in living room and bedroom 3 (study), with gurjun hardwood in dining room and hall, with softwood in bedrooms 1 and 2 and with ceramic tiles in kitchen and bathroom. *Windows:* hardwood; south windows of living room double-glazed with Insulight.

HEATING. Floor panel heating throughout. A description of this installation, which is entirely automatic, is given in the *Appendix* on page 107.

AREAS. Total area: 1,650 sq. ft. Living room 24 ft × 15 ft; dining room 13 ft × 10 ft; kitchen 15 ft × 11 ft; bedroom 1 15 ft × 14 ft; bedroom 2 13 ft × 9 ft; bedroom 3 13 ft × 11 ft.

COST. £5,362. Approximately 65s. per sq. ft.

Right: the dining room looking towards the built-in fitting with hatch and door leading to the kitchen. Below: the house from the north-west. In the angle formed by the two wings there is a sun terrace with an outside fireplace.

Above: the living room of the house near Moira, Northern Ireland, designed by E. W. Beaumont. The double-glazed sliding windows open onto a terrace and look out across part of the garden towards the trees which border the road on the south. Below: another view of the living room looking towards the brick-faced fireplace wall at the west end. The built-in cupboards are used for storing cocktails, a radio, a gramophone and records. The floor has a granolithic finish, with a surround of hardwood, and is close carpeted.

designed by **ERNÖ GOLDFINGER**

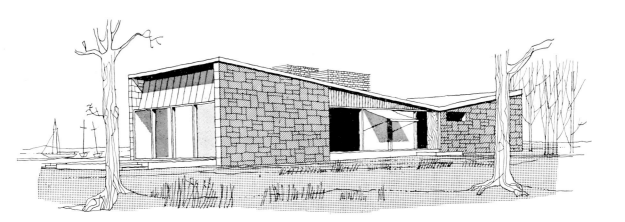

AT PRESENT BEING BUILT on a thickly wooded site, which is being partly cleared of oak trees to allow for building, this house overlooks Chichester Harbour. There are views across the water to the north, and to the west overlooking the landing stage for the owner's yacht. In the drawing above by Gordon Cullen the house is seen from the west. It is planned in two distinct parts—for day-living and for sleeping, with bathrooms and cloakrooms dividing the two areas. Dining space, living space and hall can be thrown into one. In the centre is a boiler room, some five feet below the level of the house, with a tank room above.

CONSTRUCTION. Hollow construction with brick outside and light-weight concrete slabs inside. Internal partition walls of light-weight concrete. All walls to have plaster finish. *Roof:* wooden rafters, woodwool, skim coat of plaster and 3-ply felt. *Floors:* hardwood in reception rooms and bedrooms; blue quarries in hall and passages; asphalt tiles in kitchen, bathrooms, etc. *Ceilings:* plaster on plasterboard; some ceilings of plywood.

HEATING. Oil-fired heating with radiators.

AREA. Total floor area: 1,792 sq. ft.

COST. Approximately £5,400. Approximately 60s. per sq. ft.

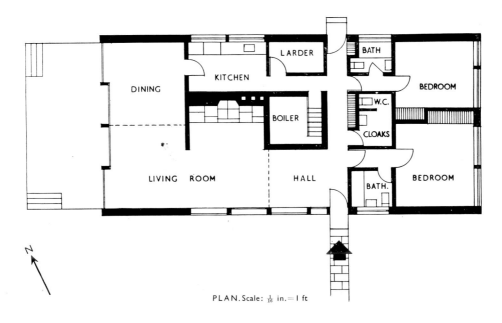

PLAN. Scale: $\frac{1}{16}$ in.=1 ft

designed by **SANDON AND HARDING**

Above: the house from the south. Below: the living room.

A LARGE LIVING AREA and full benefit of views to south-east and north-west were required when this house was planned for the owners, an elderly couple. The T-shaped plan has these advantages: (1) bedrooms are grouped in one wing and receive the morning sun; (2) economy in plumbing results from the bathroom and kitchen being adjacent; (3) the bedroom wing obscures from view another house to the east, serves as a shield against the easterly winds and forms a sun-trap for the loggia placed in the angle where the two wings join; (4) the living area separates the garden from the drive; (5) when looking from the living room windows a focal point is made of a fine lime tree to the south. As required by the owners, the elevations are treated in a traditional manner. The house was built in 1953.

CONSTRUCTION. Cavity walls with multi-coloured facing bricks; inner skin of high grade clinker block for thermal insulation. 9 in. outer skin of gable walls in English garden bond. *Roof:* timber-framed, felted and covered with dark brown concrete pantiles. *Floors:* solid concrete with various finishes, including Accotiles in kitchen and bathroom (which also has glazed wall tiles from floor to ceiling). *Windows:* E.J.M.A. wood casements of $2\frac{1}{4}$ ft unit width.

HEATING. Domestic hot water and central heating from automatic oil-fired installation. Open fire in living room. Cooking by electricity.

AREAS. 2,020 sq. ft including garage. Living/dining room $32\frac{3}{4}$ ft × $15\frac{1}{2}$ ft; kitchen 12 ft × 11 ft; main bedroom $15\frac{1}{2}$ ft × 12 ft.

COST. £4,992, including garage, porch, fuel store and covered way; excluding drive, fencing and gates. 49s. 5d. per sq. ft. (The relatively high cost per sq. ft was largely due to the heating and hot water installation.)

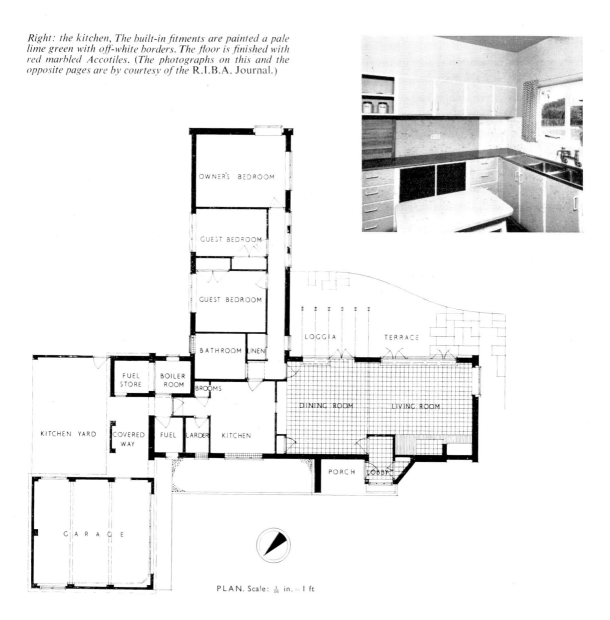

Right: the kitchen, The built-in fitments are painted a pale lime green with off-white borders. The floor is finished with red marbled Accotiles. (The photographs on this and the opposite pages are by courtesy of the R.I.B.A. Journal.)

OWNER'S BEDROOM

GUEST BEDROOM

GUEST BEDROOM

BATHROOM LINEN

FUEL STORE

BOILER ROOM

BROOMS

LOGGIA

TERRACE

DINING ROOM

LIVING ROOM

KITCHEN YARD

COVERED WAY

FUEL

LARDER

KITCHEN

PORCH

LOBBY

GARAGE

PLAN. Scale: $\frac{1}{16}$ in. = 1 ft

Left: the entrance front of the house at Fornham All Saints, near Bury St Edmunds, from the north-west. This house received the annual award in Class A (residential buildings) made by the West Suffolk County Council in 1953, when it was built. The assessor commended the care taken in the detailing, and the quality of the workmanship and finish. The roof is pantiled, and the walls are either faced with multi-coloured pinkish-brown bricks, or with plaster rendering— a combination of brickwork and plaster which gives to the house the traditional Suffolk domestic character which the owners required.

31

designed by **POWELL AND MOYA**

A general view from the south.

STANDING 550 feet high on the sandstone ridge that runs parallel to the North Downs, the house has a magnificent forty-mile view across the Weald. The site, steeply sloping, has access from the north. The house was built in 1954.

The clients required a garage for two cars, and outside storage space. This, and the desire to make the most of the view, gave the design its most striking feature: a garage built on the roof, since one built at ground level would have been impracticable because of the slope. The storage space has been placed in the wedge left between garage, house and hillside, and a passage and stairway lead from the garage to the house. Dining room, kitchen, living room, hall and bedroom wing are all at different levels and express the slope of the site internally.

CONSTRUCTION. Walls mostly cavity construction of $4\frac{1}{2}$ in. brick with inner skin of 4 in. insulating concrete blocks. East corner of living room, and garage, constructed of 4 in. concrete blocks faced with cedar boarding on battens. *Roofs:* main roof of precast prestressed clay 'planks' with hollow clay filling pots and *in situ* concrete topping, insulated on top with 1 in. cork slabs waterproofed with patent roofing felt laid level; roof finished with blue-grey granite chippings; roof of garage and boxroom of t. and g. boarding and patent roofing felt on timber joists. *Floors:* cement screed on surface concrete, with damp proof membrane between, standing on hardcore base, with various finishes including hardwood blocks (Muhuhu) in living room and hall.

HEATING. Central heating from solid fuel boiler, with electric circulating pump, in kitchen. Cooking and hot water from solid fuel cooker with immersion heater in cylinder.

AREAS. House only: 1,367 sq. ft. Outbuildings (which are within main structure): 684 sq. ft. Total area: 2,051 sq. ft. Living room $23\frac{1}{4}$ ft $\times$ 12 ft; dining room $11\frac{3}{4}$ ft $\times$ 10 ft; kitchen 16 ft $\times$ $11\frac{3}{4}$ ft; each bedroom 14 ft $\times$ 10 ft.

COST. Contract price: £4,920. Cost per sq. ft: 72s. (if based on area of house alone), and 48s. (if based on total area).

Left: the south-west elevation; the overhead garage is on the left, and next to it is the window of the box room immediately above the dining room. Above: the dining room. Below: the house from the north; brickwork is tarred or painted white.

GARDEN LEVEL PLAN
Scale: $\frac{1}{16}$ in. = 1 ft

ROAD LEVEL PLAN

STORE   STORE

DINING ROOM   KITCHEN

HALL

CLOAKS   BATHRM

BEDROOM

VERANDAH   LIVING ROOM

BEDROOM   BEDROOM

GARAGE

BOX ROOM

Above: looking from the kitchen hatch through the dining room to the country beyond. Below: the magnificent view seen through the south-east window of the hall.

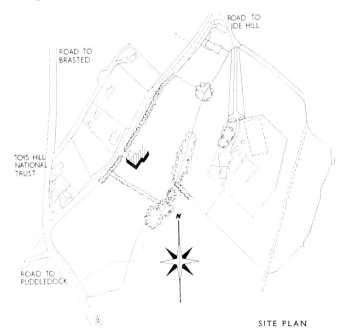

ROAD TO
DE HILL

ROAD TO
BRASTED

TOYS HILL
NATIONAL
TRUST

ROAD TO
PUDDLEDOCK

N

SITE PLAN

Looking from the dining room through the sliding windows of the living room beyond. Walls and ceilings are plastered and painted, or distempered, white.

designed by **LIONEL BRETT**

At top: the house from the south looking towards the front door. On the left is the window of the greenhouse. Right: the living room; beyond the fireplace, to the left, is the study on a higher level and, to the right, the doorless entrance to the hall. The fact that the house was to have floor panel heating originally suggested a one-storey building, with only a boiler room at a lower level. This is beneath the study and access is by an external door in the north-west wall. The house was completed in 1954.

Above: the house from the south-west; below: the living room fireplace.

THE CLIENT, a bachelor when he first approached the architect, owned a beautiful arboretum and shrub garden where he wished to build a studio and bedroom for himself and a flat for his gardener and housekeeper. But later he married, arranged other accommodation for the gardener, and the internal layout was slightly modified. The site, the steep bank of a wooded ravine, unfortunately faces north-west. The studio and bedroom (now the living room and study) were to face the ravine, the flat (now bedrooms) was to face the sun. As the site slopes, the floor levels vary and meet at the central chimney like steps at a newel-post. The dining/kitchen group acts as a buffer between living area and bedrooms.

CONSTRUCTION. Part masonry, part timber frame structure. To meet timber shortage client's own oak and fir largely used for roof framing and wall panels. Masonry walls either two skins of Thermalite blocks or cavity brickwork. *Roofs:* oak rafters, fibre board, fir boarding and laminated felt. Car port roof cantilevered from four brick piers to allow screen walls or doors to be added later. *Floors:* external York stone terrace running through hall to dining room and service door; Kahr laminated flooring laid on sand, covering heating coils, in living room and bedrooms; lino on cement screed in kitchen, bathroom and cloakroom. *Windows:* softwood frames; mullions of living room windows, front and back, are part of structural frame.

HEATING. Floor heating throughout by galvanized steel pipe coils embedded in floor slab, with thermostatically controlled Janitor boiler which also heats domestic water. Boiler flue helps heat living space. Tanks above cloakroom; circulating pipes grouped in ducts with access panels; extractor fan in ceiling above cooker. Cooking by electricity.

AREAS. 1,470 sq. ft, excluding car port and greenhouse. Living room $21\frac{3}{4}$ ft $\times 14\frac{1}{2}$ ft; study 13 ft $\times$ 11 ft; dining room and kitchen $21\frac{1}{2}$ ft $\times$ $14\frac{3}{4}$ ft; bedroom 1 18 ft $\times$ 13 ft; bedroom 2 $11\frac{3}{4}$ ft $\times$ 8 ft.

COST. Contract price: £5,026, excluding car port and greenhouse (which were later additions). 68s. $4\frac{1}{2}$d. per sq. ft.

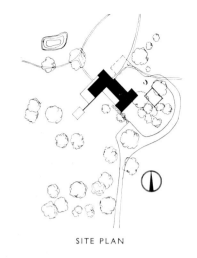

SITE PLAN

A wooded ravine—part of an existing and matured arbore-tum and shrub garden—lies to the north-west of the house at Iver Heath, Bucks. The windows of the study and living room, seen from this ravine, were planned to face across it.

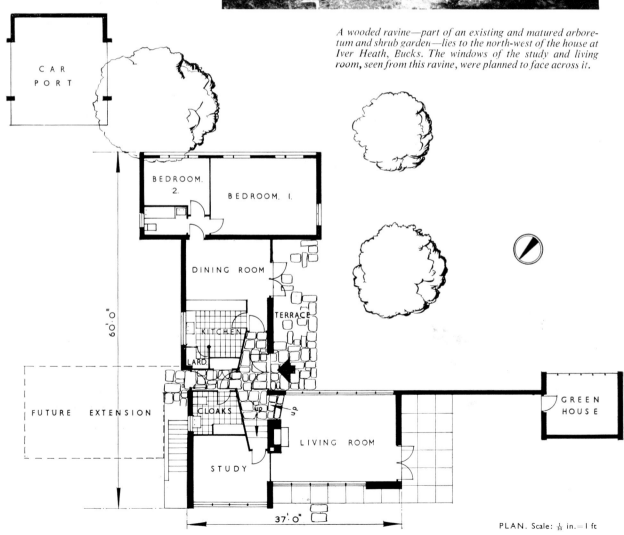

CAR PORT

BEDROOM. 2.

BEDROOM. 1.

DINING ROOM

KITCHEN

TERRACE

LARD.

FUTURE EXTENSION

60'·0"

CLOAKS

UP

UP

STUDY

LIVING ROOM

GREEN HOUSE

37'·O"

PLAN. Scale: $\frac{1}{16}$ in. = 1 ft

designed by **C. B. RATCLIFFE**

Above: the house from the south-west. Below: the house from the north-east.

THE ESSENTIAL REQUIREMENTS were an open plan, the maximum use to be made of sunlight and a heating system of the best possible kind. The site is on high ground heavily wooded. The living area is on the south side and takes in a wide view of the garden and woods, and the sleeping area is at the eastern end for privacy. To the north, the garage acts as a shield from the prevailing wind, and forms one side of a paved court to the main entrance. One large north window lights the hall where the owner (the architect of this house) has his work space. The house was built in 1954.

CONSTRUCTION. Mass concrete foundations consisting of 2 in. site concrete, damp proof membrane, 4 in. concrete and 1 in. screed finish. Cork slabs stuck to site slab round perimeter of building insulate heat flow from the floor heating. *Superstructure:* partly steel frame construction consisting of $2\frac{3}{4}$ in. diameter columns at 8 ft 3 in. centres and composite beams of 4 in. $\times$ 2 in. channels placed back-to-back. *Roof:* 5 in. $\times$ 2 in. joists covered with woodwool, slurry and three layers of bitumen felt with top dressing of limestone chippings. *Ceilings:* Swedish insulation board. *Solid walls:* 2 in. Dutch facing bricks on

outer skin, $4\frac{1}{4}$ in. hollow breeze on inner skin. *Internal partitions:* 3 in. breeze. *Windows:* metal windows infilled with 1 in. t. and g. Utile in 2 in. widths where glazing not required. *Floor finishes:* cement screed floors, close-carpeted; Marley tiles in kitchen, utility, bathroom and w.c.

HEATING. Floor panel heating throughout, with supplementary wall panels. (See *Appendix*, page 109.)

AREA. Approximately 1,310 sq. ft.

COST. Approximately £4,913, excluding garage, but including heating and all other extras. Approximately 75s. per sq. ft.

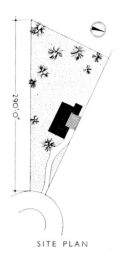

SITE PLAN

PLAN. Scale: $\frac{1}{16}$ in. = 1 ft

Two views of the living room of the house at Grovewood Close, Chorley Wood—looking east and looking west. The fireplace and chimney breast are in facing bricks, the mantelshelf is in Rosso Levanto marble and a Baxi fire is fitted. In the upper view (looking east) the double doors leading into the hall are on the left; on the right is the metal-framed window which runs along the south front and makes the most of the view across the garden. It is fitted with panels of plate glass, and the bottom units are double-glazed. In contrast to the glazing on the south side of the house, the other sides have large expanses of brickwork relieved by few windows.

The south front—an almost continuous winaow wall to obtain the maximum sunlight.

designed by **ROBERT TOWNSEND**

Above: the south side of the house from the garden. At the eastern end is a garage built at a lower level, and thus allowing space above for a playroom six feet high within the main ridge line. Access to it is by a ladder in the garage. Left: the house from the south-west. It was built in 1952.

THE ARCHITECT designed this house for himself and for his wife who is a doctor.

CONSTRUCTION. North wall, 11 in. cavity brickwork, fair faced with raked horizontal joints inside, flush joints externally. Partitions, 2 in. × 2 in. studs at 3 ft centres horizontally, and 2 ft vertically, with 2 in. woodwool slabs in the panels, both sides faced with waxed Swedish pine plywood. South wall similarly constructed but lined with building paper and 13 in. × $\frac{1}{2}$ in. vertical *oba salu* weatherboard. *Roof:* wood construction with 1 in. woodwool slabs, felt and cedar shingles. *Ceilings:* lined with beech plywood. *Floors:* solid concrete with quarry tiles.

HEATING. Embedded radiant panels with h.w. pumped from Earleymil boiler by electric pump.

AREA. Approximately 2,200 sq. ft.

COST. £4,900, including garage. Approximately 44s. 2d. per sq. ft.

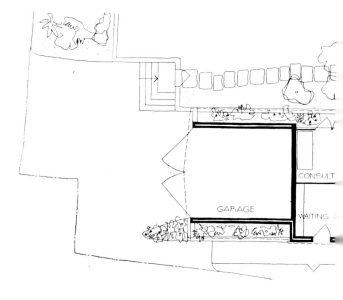

Top left: the kitchen, lit by a clerestory and separated from the living room by cupboards and a service door. Left: the dining space. Above: the living room which is turned at 45 degrees to the main axis to give maximum south exposure and an outlook along the long axis of the site. Finishes are in natural materials.

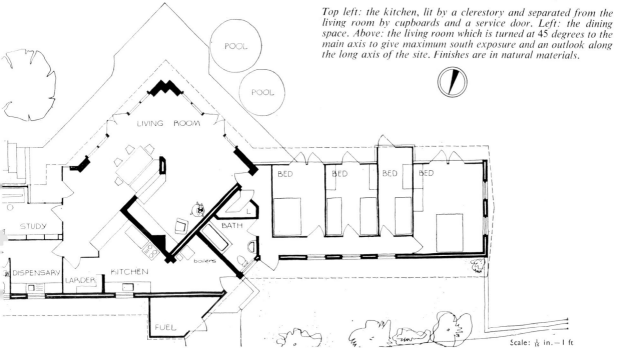

POOL

POOL

LIVING ROOM

BED BED BED BED

STUDY

BATH

L

DISPENSARY

LARDER KITCHEN

boilers

FUEL

Scale: $\frac{1}{16}$ in. = 1 ft

designed by **STEFAN BUZAS** *of* **JAMES CUBITT AND PARTNERS**

The east side and front door facing the road.

THIS SINGLE STOREY HOUSE is one of two similar houses built on a site once part of the estate of the Tollemache family, the owners of Ham House. Occupied by a partner in the firm of James Cubitt, and his family (four in all), the parents' bedroom, kitchen and living room form an open plan around a central core containing the bathroom, heating and hot water chamber and a loft above. The amount of accommodation needed within a small area posed a difficult planning and visual problem. To increase the feeling of space, the ceiling height was set at eight feet nine inches; and around the central core the number of permanent divisions were reduced to a minimum, and replaced by glass, curtains, book-shelves and cupboards. The divisions between the main rooms were not taken up to full height and the ceiling can be seen extending beyond these rooms through glazed upper portions of the walls. The central core has a low ceiling of seven feet and extends four feet above roof level for storage. The house was completed in 1954.

CONSTRUCTION. Concrete site slab and 11 in. cavity walls with clinker block inner skins and clinker block partitions. Lilac flint lime facing bricks; other faces in common Flettons with white Snowcem finish. External joinery in hardwood, with $\frac{1}{4}$ in. polished plate glass to windows. *Roof:* Benfix joists, 2 in. thermacoust slabs, $\frac{3}{4}$ in. asphalt and plasterboard ceiling. *Internal finishes:* dark green thermoplastic tiles and linoleum for floors, plastered walls, pine screen to heating chamber and varnished hardwood to external doors and windows. Curtains are pink, lemon and purple. Kitchen cupboards, wardrobes and solid doors are painted white.

HEATING. Gas-fired boiler in service core supplies hot water and hot air which is blown through a grille to heat house. Bathroom and kitchen require minimum of pipe runs; comfortable temperature in bathroom in coldest weather virtually eliminates condensation of steam.

AREAS. 1,500 sq. ft (including garage of 300 sq. ft). Living room 28 ft × 16 ft; kitchen 9 ft × 8 ft; bedroom 1 $12\frac{3}{4}$ ft × $12\frac{1}{2}$ ft; bedrooms 2 and 3 both approximately 11 ft × 11 ft.

COST: approximately £4,560 (including heating, etc.). 60s. per sq. ft.

Above: the kitchen window, the porch and, on the right, the garage, from the south-east. Below: the house from the south; on the right of the living room window is a panel of weatherboarding. The site plan, right, shows this house (at top) and the similar house built at the same time (below).

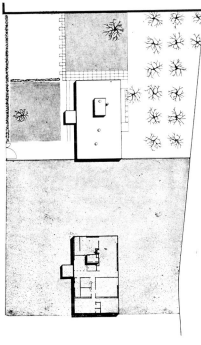

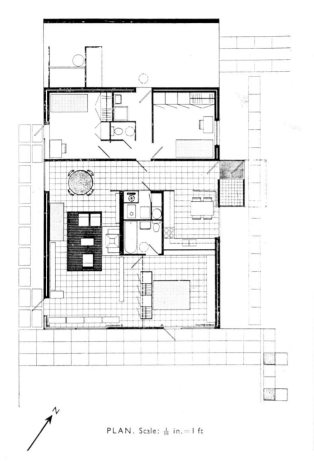

PLAN. Scale: $\frac{1}{16}$ in. = 1 ft

N

Above: the kitchen of the house at Ham Common seen from near the front door. The partition on the left has a glass top. The main bedroom is on the other side. Right: the living room, looking east towards the partition of the main bedroom. Made up of wardrobes this partition also has a panel of glazing above.

Looking south down the length of the living room to the garden beyond. Smoke is extracted from the open fireplace by means of an asbestos-lined, stove-enamelled metal hood. The hearth is in white marble with a black terrazzo inset. On the other side of the wall, on the left of the fireplace, is the central core of the house containing the bathroom, boiler and heating chamber, with a loft above which has storage space and which houses the water tank, gas meter and flushing system. Access to the loft is by a ladder in the boiler room. The bathroom is lighted by a dome-light in the roof.

47

designed by **PETER DUNHAM, WIDDUP AND HARRISON**

The main (south) elevation facing towards the road.
The house, built in 1952, stands in a ten-acre wood.

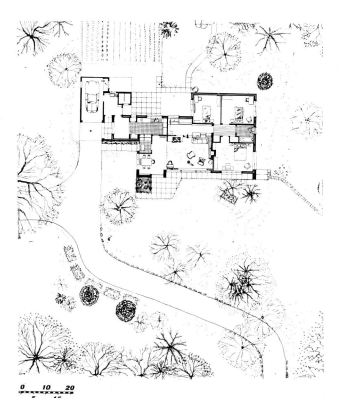

0 10 20
5 15

THE SITE slopes gently in two directions, and therefore the floors of the house change level in two places. A heating system to suit the open plan was carefully chosen.

CONSTRUCTION. External walls generally of 11 in. cavity brickwork, part of buff brown facings and part of colour washed common bricks. Walls above and below large window and over garage door of studding with cedar wood boarding. *Roof:* three-layer mineralized felt covering 2 in. compressed straw-boards on rafters. Exposed rafters in living room of 9 in. × 3 in. Agba hardwood, and of painted 7 in. × 2 in. softwood in bedrooms 2 and 3. *Floors:* solid concrete with various finishes.

HEATING. Two appliances used: (1) domestic boiler in kitchen; (2) back-boiler behind living room fireplace. Kitchen boiler serves radiators in hall, dining space, work space and a smaller bedroom, and provides domestic hot water. Back-boiler heats bathroom water and provides radiation from coil under living room window, pipes in bedroom 1 and radiator in bathroom.

AREAS. 1,363 sq. ft, including stores but excluding garage. Living/dining room and work space 30 ft × 20 ft (at widest point); bedroom 1 16 ft × $10\frac{1}{2}$ ft; kitchen $15\frac{1}{2}$ ft × $6\frac{1}{2}$ ft.

COST. Approximately £4,200, including garage, terraces, built-in cupboards and sewage disposal plant. Approximately 55s. 9d. per sq. ft.

At top: the house from the south. Centre: the main entrance; the corner is of weathered Cotswold stone. Below: (left) the kitchen; (right) the living room. The owner's work space, on the right, has a ceiling of perforated acoustic tiles.

The heating system adopted of using two standard heating appliances (as described in the text) provides central heating for the whole house (except for bedroom 2) using no more than the normal solid fuel appliances for a house of this size. Both units are independent.

designed by **FELIX WALTER**

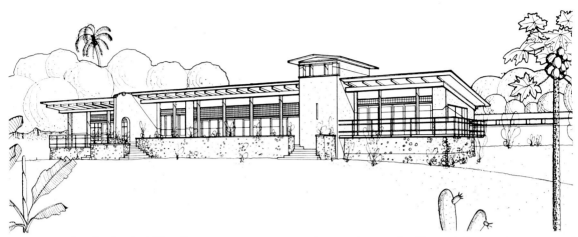

SITUATED in the bush 150 miles up country from Freetown on high land with extensive views to the south, this house was designed for a trader and his wife with a separate guests' suite. The living area is unusually large for entertaining visitors and business acquaintances on trek. Prohibitive costs of imported supplies, and loss or damage in transit, dictated the maximum use of indigenous materials.

CONSTRUCTION. Concrete foundations and floor slabs, latter having cement screed finish. R.c. columns support timber roof frames at 9 ft centres. Native fibrous mat ceilings in living area and fibreboard elsewhere, with 6 in. air space and white-painted corrugated metal roofing; air gaps sealed with mosquito gauze. Walls mainly of stabilized soil blocks rendered both sides and laid on concrete upstands and galvanized metal ant course; other walls of local stone.

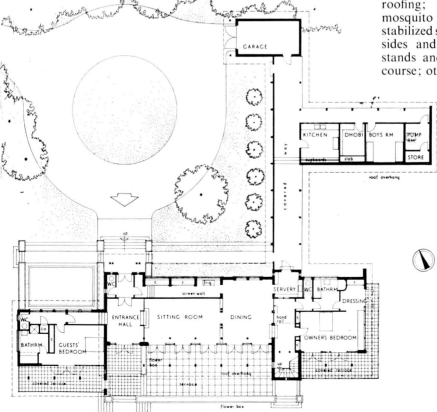

The drawing above shows a general view from the south. The water supply for the house is pumped up from a local source to tanks in the look-out tower, and drinking water is filtered and treated. A timber-fired boiler heats the hot water, for which there is a limited demand. The areas are as follows: the house (excluding verandahs and covered ways) is 2,510 square feet; the kitchen and boys' quarters, 572 square feet; the garage, 230 square feet. The estimated cost was about 26s. per square foot. (Scale of plan on left: $\frac{1}{32}$ inch equals 1 foot.)

designed by **BOOTH AND LEDEBOER**

Right: '*Acorn Hill*' *from the south-west. There are houses to the north, but fields and trees flank the other three sides.*

BUILT FOR A HEATING engineer, his wife, son and daughter, the house stands on high ground. The plan is an open one: there are no doors between hall and living room, and only a short chimney wall between living and dining rooms. The living area is on the east side and the sleeping area on the west. The house was built in 1953.

CONSTRUCTION. Cavity walls: $4\frac{1}{2}$ in. brick outer leaf finished with Tyrolese plaster and $4\frac{1}{4}$ in. Broad Acheson block inner leaf, plastered. Partitions of plastered cinder block, except in bathroom and cloakroom which have studding, plasterboard and steel lathing, plastered. North outside wall has plyglass panels to give light, privacy and insulation. *Roof:* cedar shingles with layer of fibreglass quilting below; plasterboard ceilings. *Floors:* solid concrete floor covered with secret nailed, tongued and grooved hardwood, except for kitchen, utility, cloakroom and bathroom which have Accotile floors.

HEATING. Radiant floor panel heating (see description in the *Appendix*, page 111).

AREAS. 1,478 sq. ft. Living room $17\frac{1}{2}$ ft $\times$ 13 ft; dining room 13 ft $\times$ $12\frac{1}{2}$ ft; kitchen and utility room 21 ft $\times$ $10\frac{1}{2}$ ft; bedroom 1 $14\frac{1}{2}$ ft $\times$ 11 ft.

COST. Approximately £3,700, excluding interior fitments, heating installation and some external works. Approximately 50s. per sq. ft.

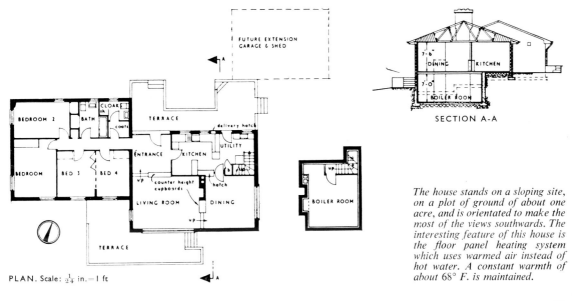

SECTION A-A

PLAN. Scale: $\frac{1}{2\frac{1}{4}}$ in. = 1 ft

The house stands on a sloping site, on a plot of ground of about one acre, and is orientated to make the most of the views southwards. The interesting feature of this house is the floor panel heating system which uses warmed air instead of hot water. A constant warmth of about 68° F. is maintained.

designed by **RICHARD SHEPPARD AND PARTNERS** (*associate architect:* **GORDON TAYLOR**)

Right: a view from the south-east. On the right is the bedroom wing and on the left the living room wing. Below: looking south along the approach to the front entrance and through the glass-walled hall. The brick wall on the right conceals the stores and will form a background for plants.

FACING the Sussex Downs, the steeply sloping half-acre site is in thick woodland which is being developed with detached houses. The house has been planned around the view to the south which is superb, and the main rooms and an outdoor living terrace all face south. Living area and bedrooms are in separate blocks connected by the hall, and as the client is a keen gardener a greenhouse accessible from the living room has been built. The house was completed in 1954.

CONSTRUCTION. 11 in. cavity walls with Dunbrik facings. Panels in white and terra-cotta Tyrolean rendering; those below dining room and greenhouse windows of rendered breeze, painted and faced with $\frac{1}{4}$ in. cast glass. *Roof:* 3-ply felt covered with spar dressing, ●n screed and 2 in. woodwool slabs, supported on 7 in. × 2 in. joists. *Floors:* 4 in. solid concrete finished with cork tiles in living room and main bedroom, quarry tiles in hall and thermoplastic tiles elsewhere. *Windows:* timber. *Doors:* natural gaboon mahogany flush doors wax polished in main rooms; elsewhere doors painted. Architects also designed other fitments in West African mahogany, obeche and painted softwood.

HEATING. Central heating by radiators in all rooms, except bedrooms 1 and 2, from Watts boiler which also supplies hot water.

AREAS. 1,511 sq. ft. Living room $21\frac{3}{4}$ ft × 11 ft, plus dining room 10 ft × $8\frac{3}{4}$ ft; kitchen $12\frac{1}{3}$ ft × 10 ft; main bedroom $20\frac{1}{2}$ ft × $11\frac{1}{4}$ ft (at widest).

COST. £3,965, including heating system, built-in furniture, fencing and external works. 53s. per sq. ft. (In addition an extra £207 was spent on pumps, etc. for the water supply.)

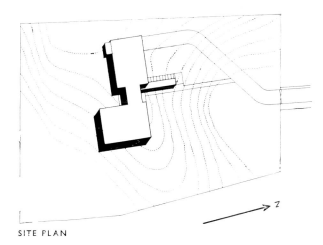

A detail of the south front showing the outdoor living terrace in front of the glass wall of the hall. As the north wall of the hall and the front door are also of glass, a through-view south to north, and vice versa, is obtained. On the right is the west wall of the bedroom wing which contains a sleeping porch. A metal staircase, yet to be built, will give access to the roof from the outdoor living terrace. The main rooms face south towards the fine view existing in that direction. The approach to the house is on the other side—the north side.

SITE PLAN

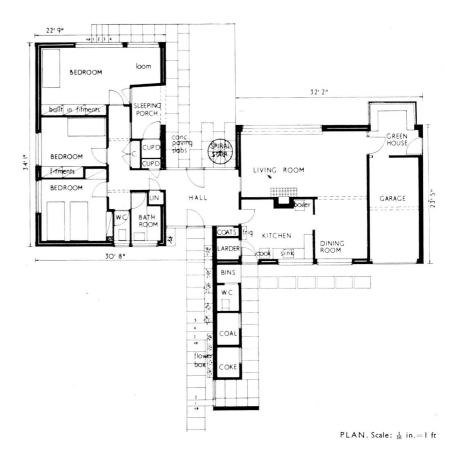

Above: the south front of the house at Storrington from the south-west. The panel below the living room window, on the left, is glass faced and covers a wall rendered olive green. On the roof above is a corner of the boarding which protects a 200 gallon storage tank. On right can be seen the sleeping porch inset in the bedroom wing.

PLAN. Scale: $\frac{1}{16}$ in. = 1 ft

designed by **DOUGLAS STEPHEN AND PARTNER** (*structural consultants: Ove Aarup and Partners*)

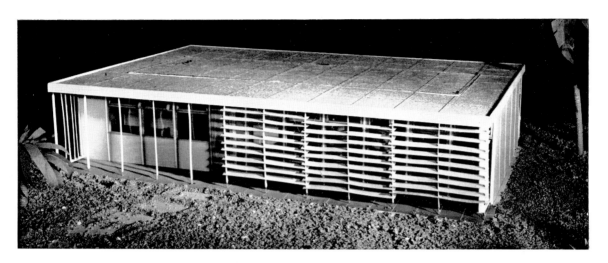

PRODUCED in 1954 by Cruden's, Ltd., the main purpose is to provide the essentials to civilized living in a hot climate. The design follows the traditional verandah type of tropical building, and it can be erected by unskilled labour assembling the fully prefabricated units on the site. The wall panels provide, within a $2\frac{1}{2}$ inch thickness, a degree of heat insulation equal to a six foot solid stone wall.

CONSTRUCTION. Twelve 28 ft 3 in. trusses span width of house at 4 ft $0\frac{1}{2}$ in. centres, each truss being bolted to pair of stanchions at 20 ft centres. Extreme ends of each truss are secured to concrete base by ties which will withstand 500 lb. pull. *Walls:* solid insulated panels $2\frac{1}{2}$ in. thick constructed on special impregnated honeycomb paper core, with U-value of 0.14. Walls faced internally and externally with resin-bonded plywood. Core surface of inner leaf has thin layer of aluminium foil. *Roof:* 4 ft sq. aluminium cells or troughs, insulation packed, carried on frames. (U-value of roof 0.08.) *Floor:* Concrete slab covered with plywood squares on adhesive-treated felt fibre. *Windows:* double glazed in teak frames.

SERVICES. Air-conditioning plant and full equipment for hot water, brackish water and fresh water supplies installed.

AREAS. Total area, including verandahs, 1,272 sq. ft. Area of accommodation, 880 sq. ft.

COST. £3,500. Cost per sq. ft: 55s.

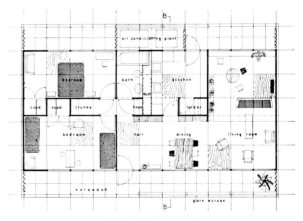

PLAN. Scale: $\frac{1}{16}$ in. = 1 ft

The drawing above shows the structural frame. The other illustrations, of a model, show (at top) the entrance front and (right) looking into the house at night through the 'brise-soleil' screening.

designed by **ABBEY AND HANSON**

The south front which faces towards a meadow beyond the garden. To the north there are woods. Windows are in softwood with double rebated frames and sashes. The covered terrace and outside terrace have flooring of York stone. The dimensions of the principal rooms are: living room 18 by 13 feet, dining room 12½ by 11½ feet, main bedroom 15 by 12½ feet and kitchen 12 by 9 feet.

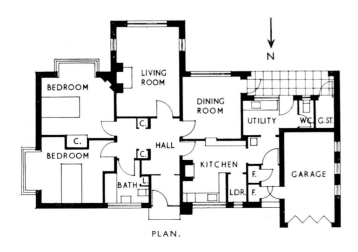

PLAN.

BUILT IN 1953 the house lies to the south of a private service road.

CONSTRUCTION. Plinth and chimneys of Crosland Hill stone laid in random courses. Walls above plinth of $2\frac{5}{8}$ in. hand-made bricks. *Roof:* dark brown interlocking tiles. *Floors:* deal boards on joists and sleeper walls in bedrooms; concrete floor with hardwood blocks on screed in lounge, hall and dining room; concrete floor with Accotile on screed in kitchen, bathroom, utility and w.c; granolithic finish in larder, fuel and garden stores and garage; quarry tiles on concrete in vestibule. *Ceilings:* plasterboard with skim coat, painted. *Internal wall finishes:* glazed wall tiles to height of $4\frac{1}{2}$ ft in bathroom, kitchen and utility; other walls plastered and painted.

AREA. 1,250 sq. ft, excluding garage, garden store and loggia.

COST. £3,500, excluding garage. Approx. 56s. per sq. ft.

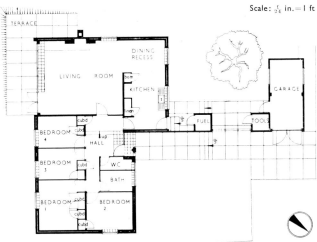

Scale: $\frac{1}{24}$ in. = 1 ft

A view from the south. The timber frame over the living room window has shingles nailed to $\frac{1}{4}$ inch chipboard. The site of three-quarters of an acre—an old kitchen garden with trees—slopes to the north-east. The house was placed as far up the slope as possible without encroaching upon too much of the space to the south. An apple tree became the centre of a courtyard formed by the outbuildings. The house was built in 1952.

A LARGE LIVING ROOM with dining space, and a kitchen lightly divided from it, was required. The budget was a strict one.

CONSTRUCTION. Cavity walls of flettons finished with Snowcem and Broad Acheson blocks. Internally walls generally distempered or wallpapered. *Roof:* timber trusses and rafters with shingles. *Floors:* solid floor slab with mahogany blocks laid in brickbond; kitchen, bathroom and lavatory have black composition tile finishes.

Windows: standard E.J.M.A. windows.
HEATING. Open fire in living room. Hot water, and heating for two radiators in living room and hall, from automatic boiler.
AREAS. House: 1,365 sq. ft. Garage and outbuilding: 210 sq. ft. Total: 1,575 sq. ft.
COST. £3,110, including garage and outbuildings. Costs per sq. ft: 42s. 6d. for house; 20s. for garage and outbuildings. Costs per ft cube: 3s. $5\frac{1}{2}$d. for house; 2s. for outbuildings.

WHEN IT IS BUILT, this house will stand on the highest point of a picturesque site of nearly two acres. Although designed for a specific site, the plan is one which would suit most requirements (except a narrow site). There are three blocks—the living area in the centre, the bedrooms on the east, and garage and stores on the west. The aspects are thus correctly served, and, whilst an entrance courtyard is formed on the north, on the other sides the most is made of views over a garden sloping down to a stream.

At top and centre: the house from the south. Below: an overhead view from the north-east. The north entrance yard, rather than being a gravel area which tends to dwarf a small house, is made of concrete paving, to take cars.

CONSTRUCTION. 11 in. cavity brick external walls. 4½ in. brick internal walls and garage walls. Walls finished internally with rough lime plaster. *Roofs:* wood construction with pantiles. *Floors:* concrete floor with vitreous tile finishes in living area. *Windows:* metal, both standard and purpose made; fixed plateglass in wood frames in living room. *Doors:* flush, with Swedish pine ply faces; mahogany front door.

HEATING. Room-heating by electrical tubular heaters throughout, and open fireplace in living room. Water heated by separate electrical thermal storage heaters in kitchen and bathroom.

AREAS. Living and bedroom wings: 1,136 sq. ft. Garage, store and fuel store: 414 sq. ft.

COST. House, including garage, stores, cesspool and all internal fittings, except heating: £3,087. Site work, drive, entrance court, paths and lay-bye on road entrance: £486. (Costs are based on tendered figures.)

Right: the house from the north. It is approached on this side by a long drive. The site was formerly an old garden full of mature trees, and the architects have re-shaped these and carried out a planting scheme. (The illustrations are of a model made by David Gray.)

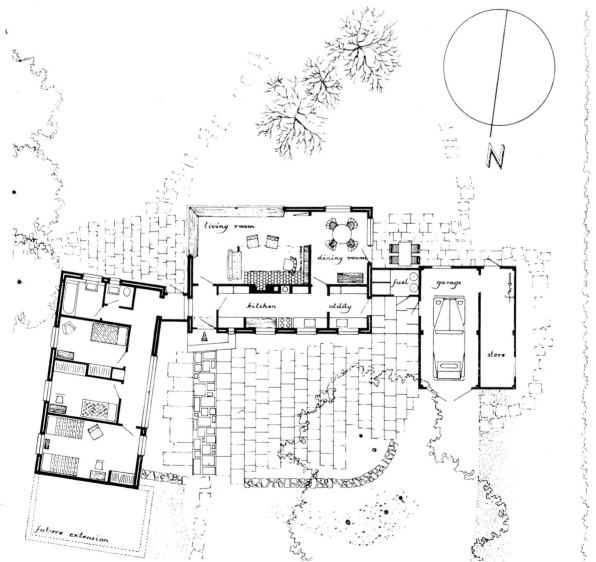

living room

dining room

fuel

garage

kitchen

utility

store

future extension

PLAN. Scale: $\frac{1}{16}$ in.=I ft

59

The west (garden) front of the house at Raynes Park, designed by Harold Bulmer and J. Ricardo Pearce. The brick walls are very pale pink in colour. The pergola, the framing to the windows and lintels are painted white. Window sashes and doors are grey, and part of the wall is rendered a dark blue. The plan of the house is an open one, entrance hall, dining room and living room being practically continuous. Only a low fireplace wall separates the dining room from the living room, which is on a lower level to benefit from the fall of the land and to obtain extra ceiling height. The house was built in 1953.

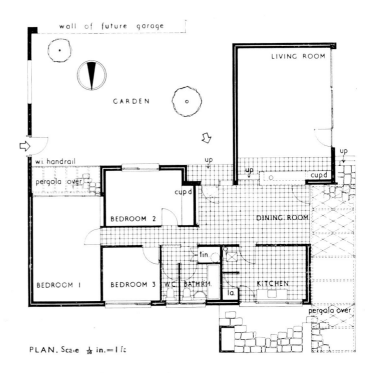

PLAN. Scale 1/8 in.=1 ft.

On the east side a plain brick wall fronts on to the road and gives privacy to the house. The view of this wall from the road is shown here. The doorway opens into a small courtyard garden which leads to the front door.

THE SITE, in a street of two-storey buildings, is a narrow one with a slight fall to the south. As the council disapproved of a bungalow on the building line, the building was set back behind this, and thus it has a free south aspect. On the side nearest the road there is a plain brick wall, enclosing a small courtyard garden through which the front door is approached. The living room is one foot lower than the remainder of the house.

CONSTRUCTION. Cavity walls: outer skin in Leicestershire facing bricks and inner skin, and partitions, in 3 in. concrete blocks. *Roof:* precast concrete beams with hollow tile infilling. *Floors:*

3 in. oak strip floor in living room; Semtex tiles in bedrooms; Ruabon heather brown quarry tiles elsewhere. *Windows:* timber framed.

HEATING. Central heating from Ideal gas-fired boiler. Immersion heater for summer use.

AREAS. Approximately 1,250 sq. ft. Living room 22 ft × 16 ft; dining room and hall 19½ ft × 10 ft; bedroom 1 17½ ft × 11½ ft; bedroom 2 15 ft × 9 ft; bedroom 3 9 ft 7 in. × 9 ft; kitchen 14¼ ft × 9 ft.

COST. Contract price, not including heating: £2,500. Total cost, including heating and extras: approximately £3,000. Approximately 48s. per sq. ft.

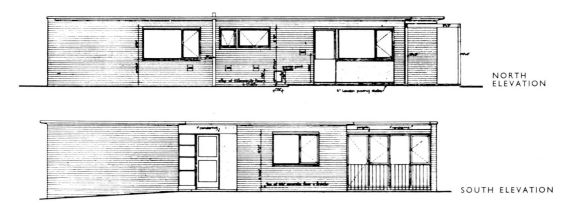

NORTH ELEVATION

SOUTH ELEVATION

61

HOUSE AT THORNHILL CREMATORIUM, CARDIFF

designed by **E. C. ROBERTS**

The north-west (approach) side. Main rooms have a south aspect.

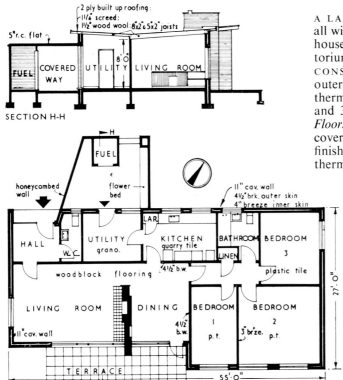

SECTION H-H

PLAN. Scale: $\frac{1}{16}$ in.=1 ft

A LARGE LIVING AREA and three bedrooms, all without built-in fittings, was required for this house for the Superintendent of the Crematorium. It was built in 1954.

CONSTRUCTION. Cavity external walls; $4\frac{1}{2}$ in. outer skin of rustic facings; 3 in. inner skin of thermalite blocks. Internal walls of $4\frac{1}{2}$ in. brick and 3 in. Thermalite. *Roof:* (see section H-H). *Floors:* 2 in. layer of blinding on hardcore filling covered with marine cement and 4 in. concrete, finished with wood blocks, quarry tiles and thermoplastic tiles. *Windows:* standard steel. Some windows have special wood frames to take standard opening sections and fixed glazing.

HEATING. H.w. from cylinder heated by solid fuel boiler. Open fire in living room; electric fires elsewhere.

AREAS. 1,230 sq. ft, excluding outbuilding. Living room $19\frac{1}{4}$ ft $\times$ 13 ft; dining room 13 ft $\times$ 10 ft; principal bedroom 14 ft $\times$ $13\frac{1}{4}$ ft; bedroom 1 $13\frac{1}{4}$ ft $\times$ 8 ft; bedroom 3 12 ft $\times$ $10\frac{1}{4}$ ft; kitchen $12\frac{3}{4}$ ft $\times$ $8\frac{1}{4}$ ft.

COST. £3,000, plus £280 for abnormal site works. Approximately 2s. $11\frac{1}{4}$d. per foot cube. Approximately 46s. $1\frac{3}{4}$d. per sq. ft, excluding site works.

designed by **BERTRAM CARTER**

The garden (south or west) front.

FOR THIS PROJECTED BUILDING an attempt has been made to design a 'universal' plan which could be used on almost any site. By changing over the garage and yard approach the entry can be reversed to suit whatever direction a site faces. The floor area is 1,000 square feet, excluding the garage and greenhouse. Features of the plan are the hall with cloakroom and wardrobe, the good storage space, the well-equipped kitchen and the bedroom corridor with bookshelves which can be treated as a library. The same architect has also designed a similar project for a two-storey building.

CONSTRUCTION. 11 in. cavity brick walls; lintols with exposed aggregate. *Roof:* wrot softwood, covered with thermacoust and felt. *Windows:* 2 ft unit standard steel; softwood sliding window to living room. *Finishes:* some walls fairfaced and some plastered; unplastered thermacoust ceilings; hardwood block floors in living rooms, screeded floors in bedrooms, tiled floors elsewhere.

HEATING. Otto fire and one radiator in living room. Electric convection warmers in bedrooms. Esse cooker and boiler.

COST. Estimated at between £2,500 to £3,000.

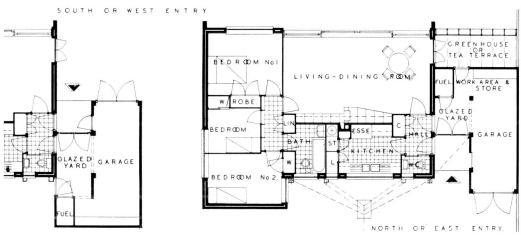

PLAN. Scale: $\frac{1}{16}$ in.=1 ft

designed by **VERNON H. LEE**

Above: the house from the south-west. The brick terrace retaining walls, in Flemish Bond with projecting headers, form a plinth for the house when viewed from down the slope. Opposite page, at top: the house from the south-east; to the right is the service entrance. Opposite page, below: the living room seen through the main south-west window.

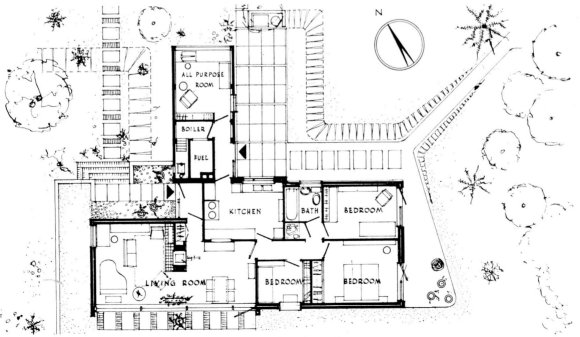

N

ALL PURPOSE ROOM

BOILER

FUEL

KITCHEN

BATH

BEDROOM

log fire

LIVING ROOM

BEDROOM

BEDROOM

PLAN. Scale: $\frac{1}{16}$ in. = 1 ft

DESIGNED and built in 1953 for the architect, his wife and two children, the house stands on the highest point of a sloping site in magnificent Chiltern woodlands. A sense of space internally and externally was achieved by contrasting the use of brick, glass, timber panels and cement rendering. The main body of the house has been planned to take exposed beams at four feet centres with asbestos roof decking units. This module governs the length of rooms.

CONSTRUCTION. External walls of load-bearing brick. External panels of $2\frac{1}{2}$ in. wide Western red cedar boarding. Internally, brick walls plastered; cedar boarding on living room walls and white glazed tiles on bathroom and kitchen walls. *Roof:* 6×3 timber joists at 4 ft centres (9×3 in lounge) with Turner's asbestos cavity decking units, $\frac{1}{2}$ in. layer insulation board set in bitumen on top-side with three-layer bitumen felt and white spar finish. *Floors:* concrete slab with damp-proof membrane, on hardcore, with various finishes.

HEATING. Ideal radiators in each room fed from Brittania boiler. Cooking and h.w. from Aga model CB cooker.

AREAS. 1,185 sq. ft. Living room 28 ft $\times$ 14 ft; bedroom 1 15 ft $\times$ 10$\frac{1}{2}$ ft.

COSTS. Site cost: £300. Site clearance: £19. Water supply: £90. Electricity supply: £47. Shell of house: £1,675. Sub-contractors, by architect: £800. Total (excluding land): £2,931. Cost per sq. ft, including fittings and services: 43s.

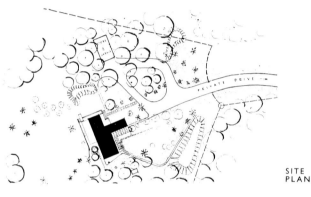

SITE PLAN

designed by **RONALD AND WALTER GREAVES**

THIS HOUSE, built in 1953 for one of the architects, his wife and three daughters, was limited in space due to building restrictions as well as economy. The site, a partially walled kitchen garden of a country house, slopes evenly down to the north. The aim in planning was to combine open living space with privacy. The plan shape is a simple rectangular one for economy and ease of building. Little storage space was planned as there is an existing barn nearby for this purpose. The architects themselves built the house with some direct labour.

CONSTRUCTION. Solid concrete foundations

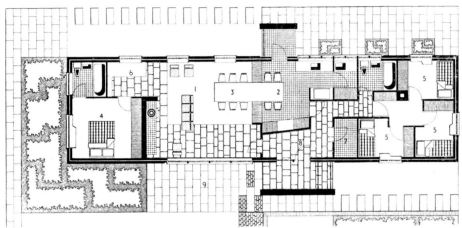

KEY TO PLAN

1. Living room
2. Kitchen
3. Dining room
4. Parents' bedroom
5. Children's bedrooms
6. Study space
7. Store
8. Entrance
9. Terrace

Scale: $\frac{1}{16}$ in. = 1 ft

Above: the house from the south-west. Brickwork is either white flints or painted with black bituminous paint. Right: the south front. The solid entrance-porch walls are rendered and painted. The external appearance of the house had to be approved by the land-owner as a condition of sale. For this reason the roof had to be a pitched one, instead of the flat one originally intended. On plan, living area and kitchen are placed centrally to separate parents' rooms at one end from children's rooms at the other.

and floor slab. Cavity brick external walls. Brick or breeze partitions. *Roof:* slate roof with wide curved zinc ridge and flashings. *Floors:* floor slab finished with wood blocks and stone in living room, quarry tiles in kitchen and bathroom and composition (for later carpeting) in bedrooms. *Internal finishes:* all ceilings and some walls painted, other walls wallpapered or left in natural brickwork.

HEATING. Heating and cooking by solid fuel. Esse cooker and water heater. Otto stove in living room. Small closed stove in lobby to heat children's bedroom.

AREA. Approximately 1,050 sq. ft.

COST. Approximately £2,750. Approximately 52s. 6d. per sq. ft.

Above: a view of the living area. The north wall is matchboarded and part of the floor is in stone. Left: the east end of this room showing the fitment containing a hatch separating the dining space from the kitchen. Built-in fitments such as this one are made of three-quarter inch blockboard, either painted, or stained and waxed.

designed by JUNE PARK

The house from the south.

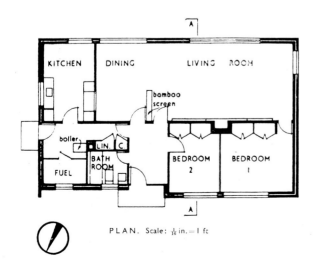

PLAN. Scale: $\frac{1}{16}$ in. = 1 ft

THERE ARE OPEN FIELDS at the back of this house, which is built on a site situated amongst some larger pre-war houses standing in a fairly rural lane. A house with a large living area and two bedrooms was required and the building was completed in 1953.

CONSTRUCTION. Traditional primrose multi-brown bricks with breeze inner skin to the 11 in. cavity wall. *Roof:* timber roof covered with brown clay pantiles with felt underlay. *Windows:* standard steel and non-standard timber. Living room window on south-east side is 12 ft × 7 ft and contains a sliding french door 5 ft wide. *Floors:* 6 in. concrete in two layers, finished with wood blocks in living room, close carpets in bedrooms, and lino elsewhere. *Decoration:* generally in distemper or emulsion paint; hatch doors and book-case of polished mahogany. Part of road façade has white Tyrolean finish.

Above: the living room with dining space beyond. Since as large a living space as possible was required, the two areas are only separated by a bamboo screen, and together they measure 35 feet in length and 13½ feet in width. Right: another view of the living room, showing the fireplace. This house at Shenfield has been planned so that it may be enlarged, if necessary, by the addition of another bedroom wing on the north side which faces towards the road. The hall would then be extended to form a link with the new wing, and bedroom 1 would become a study.

HEATING. Central heating by radiators from Ideal boiler in lobby near back door and internal fuel store. Open fire in living room. Calorifier in roof space contains electric immersion heater for summer use. To get natural circulation to radiators main flow is run at high level in roof space, with drops in four places, and returns below the floor. Almost all pipes are concealed.
AREAS. Total area: 1,112 sq. ft. Living/dining room 35 ft × 13½ ft; bedroom 1 12¾ ft × 11¾ ft; bedroom 2 11¾ ft × 9 ft.; kitchen 13½ ft × 9 ft.
COST. £2,700 (contract price). 48s. 6½d. per sq. ft.

designed by **IAN WARWICK**

The north-west wall of the study.

THE ILLUSTRATIONS are of a single-storey house which was converted in 1953 from some outbuildings belonging to an adjacent Georgian house in The Crescent, Bedford. As the site is small and narrow, the opportunity was taken to contrive long views through the house by the use of glass doors and a long corridor lit by skylights.

CONSTRUCTION. Traditional construction. New cavity walls have brick outer skin and inner skin of insulation blocks. Concrete floors finished with thermoplastic tiles, laid in diagonal pattern in hall and corridor to increase apparent width.

Provision of steps down from dining area to living room saved filling and concreting.

HEATING. Radiators in living room and bedrooms heated by water from back-boiler to living room fireplace.

AREAS. Approximately 1,425 sq. ft, excluding garages. Living/dining room $33\frac{1}{2}$ ft × 15 ft; study $16\frac{1}{4}$ ft × $11\frac{1}{4}$ ft; bedroom 1 $15\frac{1}{4}$ ft × $8\frac{1}{2}$ ft; bedroom 2 $8\frac{1}{2}$ ft × $8\frac{1}{2}$ ft; bedroom 3 $10\frac{1}{2}$ ft × $5\frac{1}{2}$ ft.

COST. Licence figure for conversion was £2,555. This includes cost of a great deal of underpinning, pulling down and re-erecting, and also the removal of dry rot.

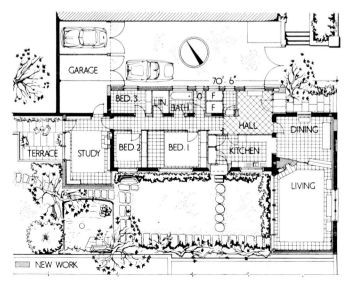

GARAGE

70'. 6"

BED. 3

LIN BATH O F F

HALL

DINING

TERRACE STUDY BED. 2 BED. 1 KITCHEN

LIVING

NEW WORK

Top left: the internal angle of the house from the west showing the outside doorway to the kitchen. Top right: the main entrance from the north-east. Centre left: the living room with the dining area to the right; walls are coloured mushroom pink, beams are grey, ceiling and paintwork white, and the floor an azure blue. Centre right: the hall and corridor looking north-west; walls are yellow, the ceiling blue and white, and the glass shelves displaying pewter have a venetian-red frame.

PLAN. Scale: $\frac{1}{24}$ in. = 1 ft

designed by **HARRY S. BARNES**

FIRST FLOOR PLAN

The house in Chadwick Lane, Heywood, Lancs, from the south-east. On the left, partially obscured by the terrace screen, is the window to the principal bedroom. In the centre are the large windows with glazed doors to the living room which open out onto a terrace of concrete paving. On the extreme right the window to the upstairs studio can be seen.

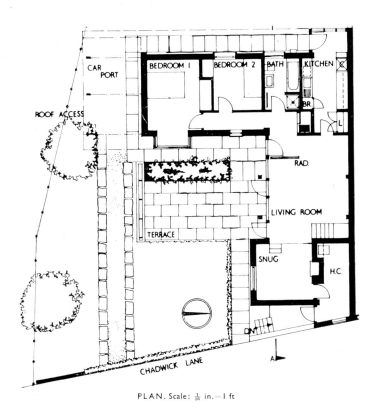

PLAN. Scale: $\frac{1}{16}$ in.=1 ft

THE ARCHITECT designed this house for his own use, and he and his staff carried out much of the actual building work, during their spare time. It is planned on one floor, except for the room known as the 'snug' at lower ground level with the studio above it. When building the house in 1953 inexpensive bricks were in short supply, and brickwork therefore was costly.

CONSTRUCTION. *Foundations:* concrete footings generally. Concrete slab to heating chamber and 'snug' has bituminous sandwich damp proof course. Timber post foundations of 1½ in. diameter steel rods set in concrete with collar and steel plate to keep foot of posts clear of ground. *Walls:* brick construction finished with golden-brown sand-faced rustic bricks. Timber main frames to living room. Large area of plate-glass with western red cedar boarding externally on south side of living room. West wall lime cement rendered. Stramit lining to north wall for heat insulation. *Roof:* asbestos cement cavity decking with 2-ply bituminous roofing. *Floors:* concrete on hardcore base finished with thermoplastic tiles in living room, quarry tiles in kitchen and bathroom, and floor boarding in 'snug'. *Ceilings:* cavity decking, painted, in living room; oak joists and ½ in. insulation board in 'snug'.

HEATING. By coils laid in concrete floor, and one radiator in main living space. Only fireplace at lower ground floor level in the 'snug'.

AREAS. 950 sq. ft, excluding car port. Living room 17 ft × 14 ft; 'snug' 11ft × 9 ft; kitchen 15 ft × 8½ ft; bedroom 1 12 ft × 9½ ft; bedroom 2 9 ft × 9 ft.

COST. £2,547. including drains. 58s. per sq. ft.

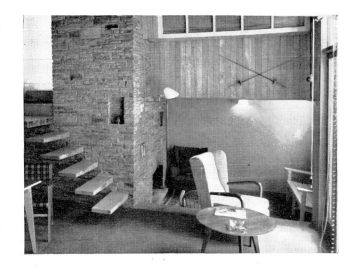

At top: the living room looking towards the 'snug' which is on a lower level beneath the studio. The fireplace and chimney stack were built of quarry waste random rubble. These rubble slabs were pitch-faced on the site by untrained bricklayers, but the result was highly successful. The steps by the fireplace lead up to the studio, and the architect himself cast these in reinforced 'fondu'. Above: looking northwards through the terrace screen towards the french windows of the living room.

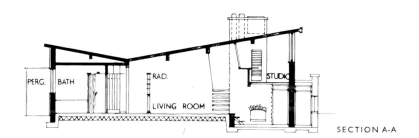

SECTION A-A

designed by **IAN WARWICK**

Above: the south front which has a view over the Kentish hills in the distance. Right: the south-east corner showing the 4½ inch brick wall screening the terrace. The total area is 987 square feet. Room dimensions are: living room 13¼ feet by 23 feet; dining recess 9½ feet by 6¾ feet; kitchen 13¼ feet by 6½ feet; bedroom 1, 12¼ feet by 10½ feet; bedroom 2, 11¾ feet by 10½ feet; bedroom 3, 10½ feet by 9 feet.

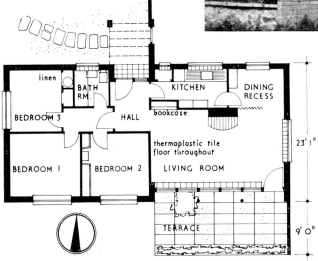

BUILT in 1953 for three elderly ladies, a fairly open plan was asked for, but bedrooms and bathroom had to be as secluded as possible.

CONSTRUCTION. 11 in. cavity brick walls; timber roof; concrete floor finished with thermoplastic tiles. Rooms plastered internally and finished with emulsion paint.

HEATING. Slow combustion stove in living room; gas wall-radiator in hall; thermostatically controlled radiators elsewhere. H.w. by multi-point gas heater.

COST. Contract price: £2,500. Approximately 51s. per sq. ft.

designed by **WALTER GREAVES**

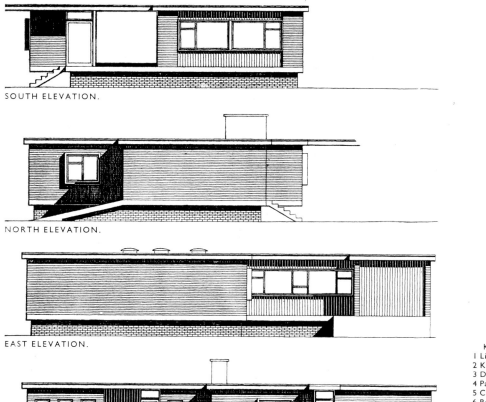

SOUTH ELEVATION.

NORTH ELEVATION.

EAST ELEVATION.

WEST ELEVATION.

KEY TO PLAN
1 Living room
2 Kitchen
3 Dining room
4 Parents' bedroom
5 Children's bedroom
6 Boiler room
7 Garage
8 Greenhouse
9 Kitchen yard
10 Formal plants
11 Terrace
Scale: $\frac{1}{24}$ in. = 1 ft

THE PROBLEM WAS to build a house for four people in a small walled site with the ground floor three feet above ground level because of the danger of flooding. The house is placed in one corner to leave space for a garden, and to link it to an existing greenhouse which will serve as an extra room. Planning is open as the house, when completed, will have floor heating.

CONSTRUCTION. Cavity walls generally. Timber framed and faced panels above and below long windows. *Roof:* flat timber roof with woodwool slabs and bituminous felt finish. *Internal finishes:* some walls left in natural brick, remainder plastered; insulating board ceilings; screeded floor finishes; tiles in kitchen and children's room. AREA. 1,000 sq. ft.

COST. £2,500. Approximately 50s. per sq. ft, plus central heating.

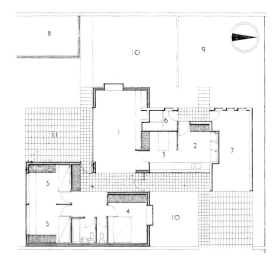

designed by **M. WALLIS**

Above: the house from the south-east. The site was once the terraced garden of a Victorian house. Right: the living room looking north towards the passage leading to the front door. Through the grille, on the right of the doorway, hot air is blown into the room from the heating system installed behind the wall. The walls are lined with plywood.

PLACED ON THE HIGHEST part of a steeply sloping site, the house has a fine view to the south-west. For economy the plan is rectangular in shape, and the roof construction was simplified by the use of single length beams laid across a spine wall (of $4\frac{1}{2}$ in. bricks) placed equidistant from the two outside walls. Warmth was important and, to keep a constant temperature of 65° F., the heating system and insulation were carefully planned. Windows were double glazed, walls lined with plywood and floors covered with cork tiles. The thermal insulation was based on the recommendation of the British Research Station's *Digest No. 16*.

CONSTRUCTION. Foundations of edge beam and 9 in. short bored piles. External walls of 9 in. Flettons rendered with grey Culamix and lined internally with 6 mm. West African mahogany plywood screwed to battens on glass wool insulation. Partitions of 3 in. clinker block, plastered. *Roof:* Casco pre-cast concrete joists with infiller clinker blocks, 1 in. screed with $\frac{1}{2}$ in. insulation board laid in bitumen, 3-ply felt and granite chippings. *Ceilings:* plasterboard. *Floors:* 5 in. concrete slab, screeded and finished with cork tiles coated with plastic (to eliminate polishing).

HEATING. Weatherfoil heating system consisting of a convector battery run parallel to indirect cylinder and warmed by thermostatically controlled coke boiler. Installation is placed in centre of house. Electric fan sucks in cold air at low level, forces it through the battery, and discharges it at height of $4\frac{1}{2}$ feet in two directions, to warm both halves of house. Advantages of system are short warming-up time and low running cost.

The house from the south-west.

The house was built by the architect for himself in 1953 and, after occupying it for a year, he has these remarks to make:—(1) The heating is very satisfactory except that in the coldest weather, there is a tendency for the air to become stratified. This may mean a difference of up to 10° F. between floor and ceiling. (2) The insulation is satisfactory, especially the plywood linings which are also decorative. (3) The running cost for hot water and heating was £30 for one year. (4) The plastic used on the cork tile floors was easy to clean but lost sheen in areas of heavy wear.

AREAS. 1,000 sq. ft., excluding garage. Living room 23 ft × 12 ft; kitchen 13 ft × 9 ft; bedroom 1 18 ft × $12\frac{1}{2}$ ft; bedrooms 2 and 3 12 ft × 12 ft.

COST. £2,400, excluding garage. 44s. per sq. ft.

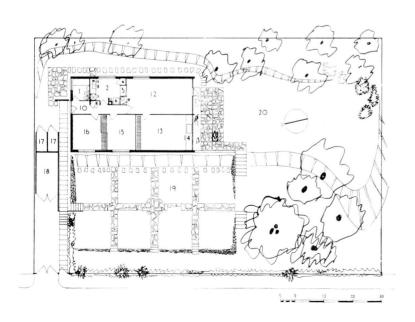

KEY TO PLAN
1. Bathroom.
2. Kitchen.
3. Sink.
4. Larder.
5. Built-in cupboards, dining hatch.
6. Boiler.
7. Gas cooker.
8. Meter cupboard, storage.
9. Heating cabinet, calorifier, water tanks.
10. Entrance lobby.
11. Refuse hatch.
12. Living/dining room.
13. Main bedroom.
14. Built-in dressing-table.
15. Bedroom.
16. Bedroom.
17. Storage.
18. Garage.
19. Existing rose garden.
20. Lawn.

designed by **SLATER, UREN AND PIKE**

The house, built in 1954, from the south-west.

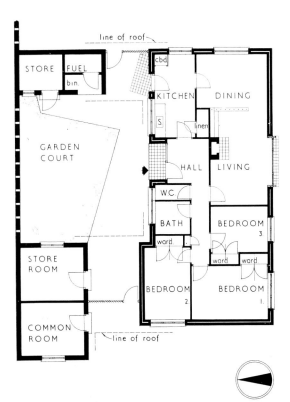

PLAN. Scale: $\frac{1}{16}$ in. = I ft

THE GENERAL CHARACTER of this house for a schoolkeeper had to be in keeping with the main design for the approach to the new school at Kidbrooke. The requirements governing the plan were: (*a*) supervision of the school's main entrance (south) from the living room; (*b*) privacy for the owner's garden court; (*c*) the inclusion of a common room (office) and cleaners' store; (*d*) the cleaners to be able to pass through from the road without entering the school's main gates.

CONSTRUCTION. 11 in. cavity walls faced with Leicestershire wire-cuts, and hollow pot internal skin. Spine wall in $4\frac{1}{2}$ in. brick; other partitions in clinker block. *Roof:* monopitch roof (to simplify rain-water drainage and to avoid cost of screeding to falls) of 5 in. reinforced concrete with 1 in. woodwool insulation and 3-ply felt roofing with green mineral finish. *Floors:* concrete floor slab with Accotiles in various colours. *Walls and ceilings:* plastered and painted; walls of bathroom and w.c. in grey Cemglaze on cement rendering.

HEATING. Ideal Neo-fire with back-boiler in living room supplying hot water and radiators in dining recess and hall. Electric fires in bedrooms.

AREA. 903 sq. ft.

COST. Approximately £2,350 (excluding items appertaining only to main entrance design or to common room and store). Approximately 47s. 11d. per sq. ft.

designed by **TAYLOR AND CROWTHER**

The south elevation. A timber glazed swing door opens into the lounge and dining room. Windows are standard metal casements and, for economy, their sills consist of two courses of slates.

THE APPROACH IS FROM a road to the north, from which the house stands back about a hundred feet. The site slopes slightly from south to north. The accommodation that was required is shown on the plan (left); a combined lounge and dining room was asked for, and it was stipulated that the larder should be large as well. The house had to be reasonably low in cost and economical to maintain and heat. It was built in 1953.

CONSTRUCTION. 10 in. concrete cavity walls. *Roof:* timber roof, at 30 degrees pitch, covered with asbestos slates; flat roof of garage covered on top of joists with Gypklith and Ruberoid finish. *Floor:* 4 in. concrete on 4 in. hardcore. *Internal finishes:* walls plastered and decorated white; all paintwork flat white; mahogany block floor and light blue ceiling with recessed lighting in lounge/dining room. The lounge furniture was designed by Robin Nance.

HEATING. Central heating by radiators.

AREA. 942 sq. ft, excluding garage and fuel stores.

COST. Contract price: £2,328. Cost per sq. ft: approximately 43s.

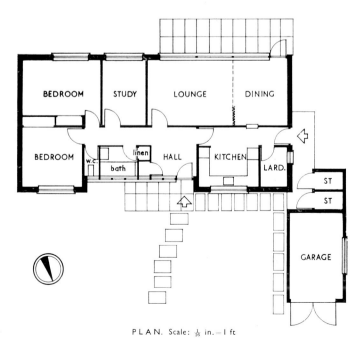

PLAN. Scale: $\frac{1}{16}$ in. = 1 ft

SHIPP RESIDENCE, SUTTON, SURREY

designed by **KATZ AND VAUGHAN**

The north front which faces towards the garden. The site is a long narrow one measuring 320 feet by 53 feet, and the site plan is illustrated below.

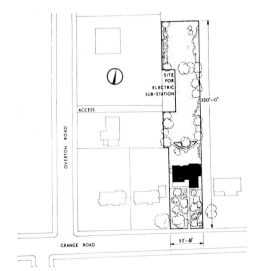

THIS IS A two-bedroomed house which faces south and north, and the living room has been planned to face south. The site is in a quiet road and the house is set seventy feet back from the pavement. It was built at Sutton in 1950.

CONSTRUCTION. Brick walls finished with rough-cast. *Roof:* pitched roof covered with Marley tiles. *Floors:* solid concrete floor finished with teak wood blocks and tessellated tiles.

HEATING. Central heating with an Ideal boiler.

AREAS. 1,050 sq. ft. Living room $20\frac{3}{4}$ ft $\times$ $15\frac{1}{2}$ ft, plus dining recess $8\frac{1}{4}$ ft $\times$ 9 ft; bedroom 1 17 ft $\times$ $12\frac{1}{4}$ ft; bedroom 2 15 ft $\times$ $12\frac{1}{4}$ ft; kitchen $12\frac{1}{4}$ ft $\times$ $9\frac{1}{4}$ ft.

COST. £2,300. Approximately 43s. $9\frac{1}{2}$d. per sq. ft.

SOUTH ELEVATION

NORTH ELEVATION. Scale: $\frac{1}{24}$ in.=1 ft

The entrance front of the house at Sutton, designed by Katz and Vaughan, viewed from the pathway on the south side which leads from the road to the front door. The house stands back 70 feet from the road.

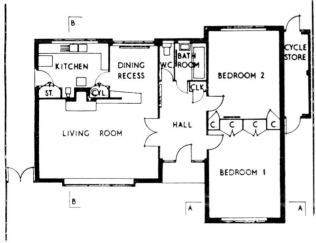

PLAN. Scale: $\frac{1}{16}$ in. = 1 ft

designed by **MICHAEL MEACHER**

The house from the south-east. It has two wings; on the right is the bedroom wing, and at right angles is the wing containing the living rooms. The garden store is on the left. The approach to the house is from a road to the west.

BUILT in 1952 this house stands on a well-wooded site, and it is planned with two wings. The western one contains the living rooms and the eastern one contains the bedrooms. Owing to the slope of the site, it is built on four levels. The south end of the living room is on the lowest level, the remainder of the living room, the dining space and kitchen are on a second level, the hall is on a third level and the bedroom wing is on the highest level.

CONSTRUCTION. External walls of either load-bearing 11 in. cavity construction, with outer skin 4½ in. brick and inner skin 4 in. blocks, or 9 in. brick clad externally with cedar weather-boarding. *Roof:* covered with 2 in. woodwool slabs on timber joists at 2 ft centres.

AREAS. 950 sq. ft. Living room 30 ft × 11 ft at its widest; bedroom 1 13 ft × 10 ft; bedroom 2 10 ft × 8½ ft; kitchen 9 ft × 7 ft.

COST. Contract price: £2,200. Approximately 46s. per sq. ft.

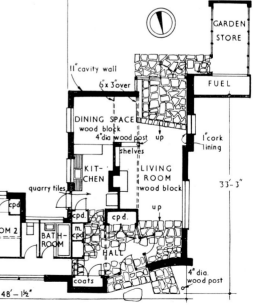

PLAN. Scale: $\frac{1}{16}$ in. = 1 ft

82

Above: the house at Welwyn Garden City, designed by Michael Meacher, seen from the road on the west side of the site. On the right is a garden store faced with cedar weather-boarding on timber studding. The windows on this side of the house light the living room which measures 30 feet by 11 feet at its widest. Round the left end of the house (the north-west corner) is the porch and front entrance, and the left-hand illustration shows this corner viewed from another angle. The site of this house, which possesses some beautiful trees, slopes slightly from north-east to south-west, and use is made of this slope to build the house on four different levels, the bedroom wing on the east being on the highest level.

At top: the north side of the house at Walberswick. The only window breaking this façade gives a north light to the owner's studio. The house was planned on one floor to enable the owner, an artist disabled in the war, to reach all parts of it in his wheel-chair. Centre: the south side. The projecting wing on the left screens the house from the south-westerly winds, and it is a part of the two-bedroom unit, containing the bathroom, planned on the west side of the house. Right: the living room looking east. The house was built in 1950.

TO THE SOUTH is an unobstructed view over farmland and marshes to the North Sea beyond. To the north the road bounds the site of over a quarter of an acre, which is exposed on all sides except the east which is protected by a dense hedge. A building line of 40 feet—about a third of the depth of the site—was imposed by the County Council. On plan the main entrance, studio recess and sitting and dining areas are subdivided unobtrusively by screens and fittings, thus giving a sense of space in a house which, for financial reasons, has a limited floor area. All doors—there are as few as possible—are 35 inches wide to take the owner's wheel chair, and a covered way enables him to reach the garage.

CONSTRUCTION. Main external walls of 11 in. cavity, fletton bricks. Internal walls and partitions of 4 in. fletton bricks and breeze blocks. *Main roof:* one-way pitch, supported by sawn rafters with, above, two layers of $\frac{1}{2}$ in. insulation board, deeply lapped non-tearable roofing felt, counter and tiling battens and red pantiles. *Flat roofs:* two layers of $\frac{1}{2}$ in. insulation board resting on ceiling joists and rough boarding covered with 3-ply felt. *Floors:* mainly t. and g. deal on breeze resting on 6 in. waterproof slab with continuous membrane between; quarry tiles in kitchen; polished cork tiles in bathroom and one bedroom. *Wall finishes:* stone paint, light buff-peach colour on brick walls externally; walls of

Above: the living room viewed from the kitchen and looking towards the studio recess in the background. The room is close-carpeted in grey and has exposed sawn roof rafters to give an increased sense of height.

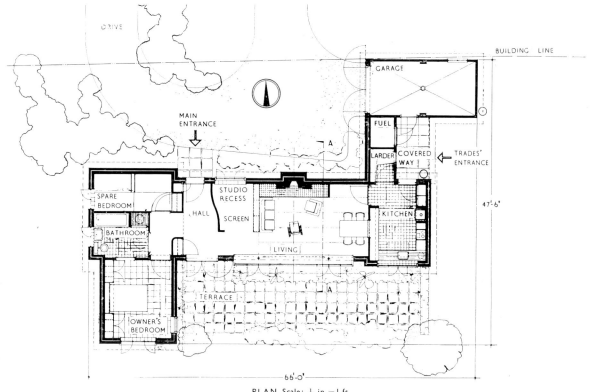

PLAN. Scale: $\frac{1}{16}$ in. = 1 ft

kitchen (east and south) and chimney stacks in local red facing bricks; internally walls plastered and distempered, except for kitchen and bathroom walls coated with plastic emulsion paint.

HEATING. Solid fuel boiler in kitchen heats continuous radiator beneath living room window and 10 gallon hot tank in kitchen for use of sink only. This tank also contains electric immersion heater for summer use. Feed tank is in roof space above kitchen. Electric storage in linen cupboard heats bathroom water. Ring main points throughout house for extra space-heating.

AREAS. 1,140 sq. ft. Living room 31 ft × 12 ft; owner's bedroom $13\frac{1}{4}$ ft × 12 ft; spare bedroom $13\frac{1}{2}$ ft × 6 ft; kitchen $13\frac{1}{2}$ ft × $9\frac{1}{2}$ ft.

COST. Contract price: £2,170, excluding drive. 38s. 1d. per sq. ft.

At top: the living room window, 20 *feet wide, of the house at Walberswick. Set in a precast concrete projecting frame, the upper members are hung from twin R.S.J's. Above: the studio recess.*

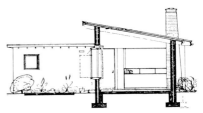

SECTION A-A

designed by **ERNÖ GOLDFINGER**

Above: the east front. This house for the caretaker of a school in Brandlehow Road was built in 1951 for the London County Council. Below: the west front; the approach from the road is on this side.

THE APPROACH is from Brandlehow Road which runs on a north to south axis on the west side of the site.

CONSTRUCTION. 11 in. cavity brickwork with Hamhill brick facings. Partitions, 2 in. hollow clay blocks. *Roof:* 5½ in. Rapid pre-cast concrete units with 2 in. lightweight concrete and Ruberoid above. *Floors:* 9 in. × 9 in. cork tiles in living room; 9 in. × 9 in. Accotiles elsewhere. *Windows:* standard steel in pre-cast concrete frames.

HEATING. Solid fuel stove in living room. Domestic h.w. from Ascot multipoint in kitchen.

AREA. 842 sq. ft.

COST. £2,080. Approximately 49s. 4¾d. per sq. ft.

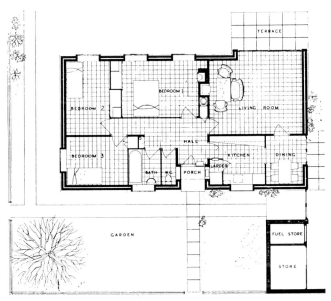

PLAN. Scale: ⅟₁₈ in. = 1 ft

Above: the house from the garden on the south-east side. Right: the house from the west. The bedrooms on this side have glazed french doors so that beds can be carried outside in the warm weather. The central portion of the roof on each side of the spine wall is a simple lean-to with spandrel windows which light the bedroom corridor on one side of the house, and the living room on the other.

SITUATED ON THE LIMESTONE RIDGE which runs from Corsham to Bath, the site slopes to the south-east and has views from north-east to north-west. A home for the owner and four children was required, as well as a building that would fit into the countryside. As a rigorous budget had to be observed, the solution was to have a simple plan, to eliminate all inessentials, to have a large living room and to use stone, wood and lime plaster. The house is planned on two sides of a spine wall of Cotswold Dale random stone—bedrooms on one side, and kitchen, living room and the main bedroom on the other. The main bedroom may later be used as a study, in which case an opening would be made in the clinker block partition to connect it to the living room. Built in 1954, it was hoped to demonstrate that a slender budget and limited space need not necessarily produce a common-place building.

CONSTRUCTION. External walls of random rubble up to 4 ft 6 in. and square-edged weather-boarding above. All stonework unplastered internally. Clinker block partitions and inner face of stud upper walls plastered in lime plaster and finished with a wood float. *Roof:* roof covered with grey asbestos cement tiles. *Ceilings:* insulating board. *Floors:* solid floors surfaced with black Accotile.

HEATING. Fireplaces with slow-burning grates. From flue of one fireplace warm air is carried to younger children's bedroom. Cooking and hot-water from Aga cooker.

AREAS. 1,100 sq. ft. Living room 19 ft $\times$ 14$\frac{1}{2}$ ft; kitchen and lobby 14$\frac{1}{2}$ ft $\times$ 7$\frac{1}{4}$ ft; bedroom 1 13 ft $\times$ 10 ft; bedroom 2 11 ft $\times$ 9 ft; bedroom 3 11 ft $\times$ 9 ft; bedroom 4 11 ft $\times$ 14 ft.

COST. Under £2,000. 36s. per sq. ft.

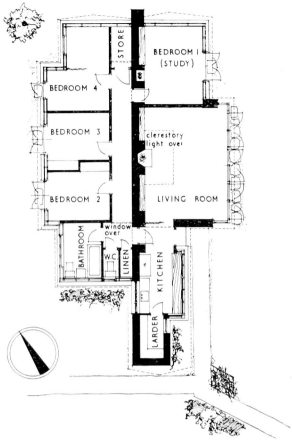

PLAN. Scale: $\frac{1}{16}$ in. = 1 ft

The living room which has large windows opening on to the garden and looking out over a good view to the south-east. On the fireplace side of the room (opposite the windows but not seen in the illustration) there is additional lighting from windows in the spandrels of the lean-to roof. The house was planned on one floor as it was felt that this was the best way to make the building—which was limited to an area of 1,100 square feet—fit into the countryside.

designed by **W. H. COLT, SON AND CO. LTD.** *in collaboration with* **A. L. OSBORNE**

THE PREFABRICATED timber building illustrated on this page has been planned and constructed by a method which has been developed into a fully modular system by Mr. Osborne for use by W. H. Colt, Son & Co. Ltd. in all the buildings they produce. A high degree of standardization of parts permits wide freedom of planning, and the client can make his own modifications to the plan selected from the series of basic designs drawn by the firm. The post, beam and panel construction is based on a three-dimensional four foot grid. Walls, partitions, roofs, floors and ceilings are made in a range of standard panels. The computed U values are as follows: roof and ceiling, 0.14; external walls, 0.13. The superstructure can be erected on a concrete raft, or on a joisted floor on sleeper walls, and owing to the simplicity of the construction houses can be erected by semi-skilled labour.

CONSTRUCTION. 3 in. framework covered both sides by $\frac{1}{2}$ in. insulation board covered by building paper, battens and cedar shingles. (Alternative material to shingles for use in a house of this type: imported hardwood boarding, laid vertically or horizontally, oiled or painted). Internally, normal finishes applied to lining of $\frac{1}{2}$ in. insulation board. Finishes that can be used include: fire-retardant treatment if required, or wood panelling, or wall tiling or plastic sheeting, etc. Prefabricated timber truss roof covered with cedar shingles. Concrete raft floor containing continuous bituminous damp proof course.

AREA. 900 sq. ft.

COST. The cost of a house of this type, in 1955, is under £2,000.

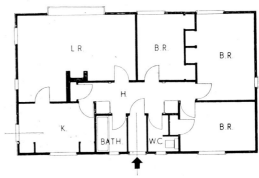

PLAN. Scale: $\frac{1}{16}$ in. = 1 ft

designed by **DENIS CLARKE HALL AND L. W. ELLIOTT**

A view from the south-west of the cottage at Greenwich. The external walls are finished with red sand-faced facing bricks and rendered panels. In the centre is the living room window which faces south.

THIS COTTAGE WAS ERECTED at the Cherry Orchard Primary School at Greenwich in 1952. The approach is from a road on the north, and to the north and east of the cottage there is a garden. The living room is planned on the south side and, covering the whole of one wall of this room, there is a window which looks across the play-ground towards the school.

CONSTRUCTION. Foundation slab of 6 in. concrete reinforced with steel mesh, with an edge beam $1\frac{1}{2}$ ft deep. $10\frac{1}{2}$ in. cavity walls consisting of $4\frac{1}{2}$ in. brick outer skin and 4 in. breeze inner skin. *Roof:* 6 in. × 2 in. joists, 1 in. boarding, 1 in. woodwool and felt. *Internal finishes:* walls and ceilings plastered and painted with emulsion paint; floors finished with thermoplastic tiles.

HEATING. Heating and hot water from Ideal Neo-fire.

AREAS. 1,150 sq. ft. Living room $17\frac{3}{4}$ ft × $12\frac{1}{4}$ ft; main bedroom 12 ft $10\frac{1}{2}$ in. × 11 ft; kitchen $12\frac{3}{4}$ ft × $8\frac{1}{4}$ ft.

COST. £1,771. Approximately 30s. per sq. ft.

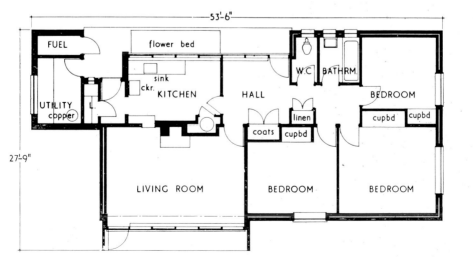

PLAN. Scale: $\frac{1}{12}$ in. = 1 ft

HAUXTON ROAD, TRUMPINGTON, CAMBRIDGESHIRE

designed by **D. C. DENTON-SMITH AND PARTNERS**

The house from the west. The specially made steel window is 22 feet by 7 feet 8 inches and is set in a reinforced concrete surround which has been poured in situ. The hand-made external facing bricks are warm buff in colour. The house was completed in 1948.

THE SITE of two and a half acres was chosen because it was near the town of Cambridge as well as the open country. (See sections A-A and B-B for constructional details.)

HEATING. Fireplace in lounge; electric panel fires in bedrooms; tubular heaters in bathroom. Cooking and h.w. by electricity.

AREAS. 1,073½ sq. ft, including garage. Lounge/dining room 28½ ft × 12½ ft; bedroom 1 17¼ ft × 10 ft; bedroom 2 11¼ ft × 10 ft; kitchen 12½ ft × 7½ ft.

COST. £1,750. Cost per sq. ft: 32s. 7⅞d.

PLAN. Scale: $\frac{1}{16}$ in. = 1

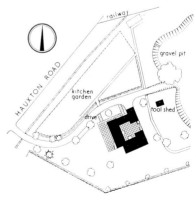

SITE PLAN. Scale: $\frac{1}{120}$ in. = 1 ft

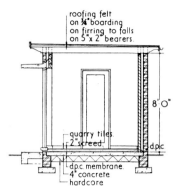

SECTION A-A.

roofing felt
on ¾" boarding
on firring to falls
on 5"x 2" bearers.

8'-0"

quarry tiles.
2" screed

d.p.c.

d.p.c. membrane.
4" concrete
hardcore

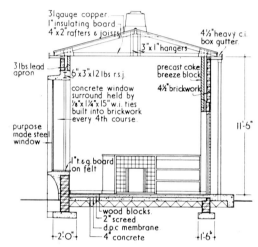

31 gauge copper.
1" insulating board
4"x2" rafters & joists

4½" heavy c.i.
box gutter.

3"x 1" hangers

precast coke
breeze block
4½" brickwork

31 lbs lead
apron

6"x 3"x12 lbs r.s.j.

concrete window
surround held by
⅛"x 1¼"x 15" w.i. ties
built into brickwork
every 4th course.

purpose
made steel
window

11'-6"

1" t.&g. board
on felt

wood blocks.
2" screed
d.p.c membrane
4" concrete

2'-0"

1'-6"

SECTION B-B. Scale: ⅛ in.=1 ft

Above: the lounge/dining room, 338 square feet, has a fireplace in the centre, the flue of which runs horizontally to the outside wall. Below: the house from the east. There are two wings, one containing the kitchen near to the dining space, and the other containing two bedrooms and a bathroom.

designed by **R. G. R. HAGGARD AND L. W. COOK**

Above: the house from the south-west. Below: the entrance front facing towards the road on the east side from which the house stands back some 48 feet. The garden extends on the west side. The illustrations on the opposite page show (left) the west end of the lounge, which has a large sliding window opening onto the garden, and (right) the hall window looking west.

THE SITE, long but only 49 feet in width, runs on an east-west axis. Existing trees were retained. The client required the lounge to face south, to be large enough for table-tennis, and to have a work room adjacent. Part of the garden, south of the lounge, was treated as an extension of the living area. The house was built in 1947.

CONSTRUCTION. External walls in a dry-mix concrete, with a continuous cavity, made by the 'Hyspecon' walling machine, which is a patent travelling form casting $2\frac{1}{2}$ sq. ft of 9 in. cavity concrete wall per filling. Internal walls 4 in. concrete. *Roof:* copper sheeting on insulation board. *Floors:* 4 in. concrete finished generally with waxed wood block floors, but with cork tiles in bathroom and bedroom. Walls and ceilings generally distempered.

HEATING. Open fires or electric heaters in rooms. Water heated by dual electric heater under draining board.

AREAS. Approximately 1,200 sq. ft. Living room 24 ft × 13 ft; study 12 ft × 10 ft; bedroom 13 ft × 11 ft; dining recess 10 ft × 5 ft; kitchen 7 ft × 6 ft.

COST. Approximately £1,650. Approximately 27s. 6d. per sq. ft.

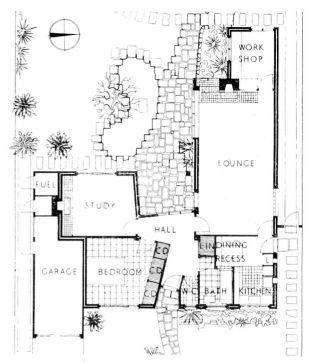

PLAN. Scale: $\frac{1}{16}$ in. = 1 ft

95

CREEVAGH, LONDONDERRY, N. IRELAND

designed by **W. H. D. McCORMICK**

PROTECTED BY trees to north and west, the house (built in 1949) has views to south and east. The site falls steeply to the south.

CONSTRUCTION. 11 in. cavity walls with concrete brick outside and 4½ in. breeze lining. Walls rough cast externally or faced with random stone rubble. *Roof:* r.c. slab on Tentest permanent shuttering, with breeze screed and asphalt finish. *Floors:* solid concrete with t. and g. boarding, wood block and tile finishes. *Windows:* steel.

HEATING and h.w. from solid fuel stove.

AREA. 900 sq. ft.

COST. £1,750. Approximately 38s. 10d. per sq. ft, and 3s. 6d. per cu. ft.

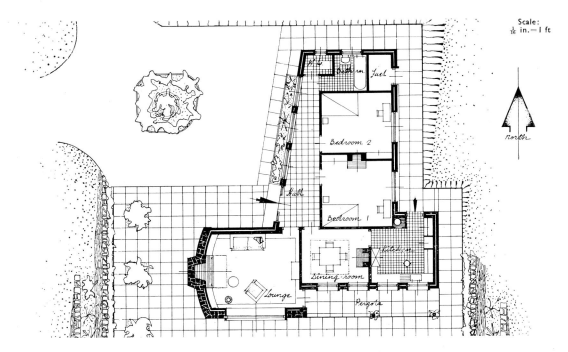

designed by **F. M. WIDDUP AND R. S. WILLIAMSON**

The south front, with the window of the living room in the centre and the front door on the right. Below: the living room. The fireplace wall is left in natural hand-made bricks, and the floor is covered with as- phalt-based 9 inch by 9 inch grey tiles.

THIS HOUSE at Redbourn, Hertfordshire, was designed by F. Macfarlane Widdup, A.R.I.B.A. (of Peter Dunham, Widdup and Harrison), and R. S. Williamson. It was constructed by Mr. Williamson for his own occupation, and the site is beside a lane just off Redbourn Common. No licence was granted originally for the house, but permission to build was given provided the work was done by the applicant himself with no paid labour. After the carcass was erected, the Local Authority granted a licence for the specialist work needed to complete the house. It was finished in 1950.

CONSTRUCTION. 11 in. cavity brick walls, rendered white externally. Chimney has sand-faced bricks with raked horizontal joints. *Roof:* timber-framed roof covered with plain tiles. *Floors and ceilings:* solid concrete floor finished with asphalt-based 9 in. × 9 in. grey tiles in living room and bedrooms 1 and 2, and 6 in. × 6 in. quarry tiles in kitchen; fibre-board ceilings. *Internal wall finishes:* fireplace wall in living room of local hand-made bricks, and other walls of living room and hall of fair-faced bricks dis-tempered white; plastered walls in bedrooms, bathroom and kitchen.

AREAS. 790 sq. ft. Living room 19 ft × 14½ ft; bedroom 1 12 ft × 11½ ft; bedroom 2 9 ft × 8½ ft; kitchen and dining space 21 ft × 7 ft (approxi-mately).

COST. £1,350, including cost of land. Some of the work was done by direct labour.

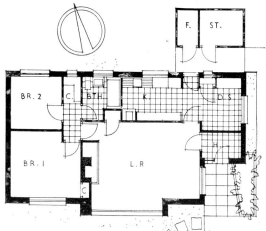

PLAN. Scale: $\frac{1}{16}$ in. = 1 ft

designed by **BEVIL GREENFIELD**

Right: the living room looking east. The ceiling follows the slope of the roof, to give additional height, and is finished with ½ inch fibre board panels, distempered.

THIS BUNGALOW was designed in 1951 for a client who required an easily run establishment with a combined living/dining room, a main bedroom heated by a continuous burning stove and a spare double bedroom. The site slopes steeply southwards from the road and there are fine views. The plan is compact, but the garage has been placed as far from the main building as the site width allows and is connected by a covered terrace. The external walls are of brick cavity construction, and the floor is solid, finished in ½ inch buff magnesite composition. Ceilings are level in the bathroom, hall, dining recess and kitchen, but in the bedrooms and living room height is gained by following the roof slopes internally. The other constructional details are shown in the sections below and opposite.

AREAS. Approximately 785 sq. ft (excluding outbuildings and garage). Living room 16 ft × 10 ft; dining space 10 ft × 6½ ft; kitchen 9½ ft × 8 ft; bedroom 1 13½ ft × 12½ ft, and bedroom 2 12 ft × 10 ft.

COST. Approximately 33s. per sq. ft, excluding outbuildings and garage.

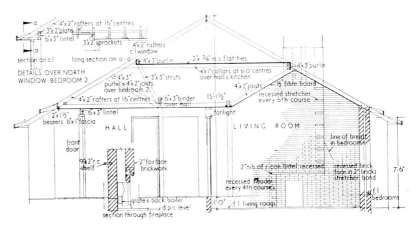

SECTION A-A. Scale: ⅛ in.=1 ft

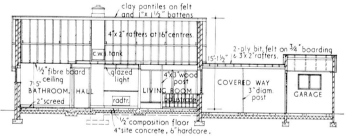

clay pantiles on felt
and 1"x 1½" battens

4"x 2" rafters at 16" centres

c.w.s tank

2-ply bit. felt on ¾" boarding
& 3"x 2" rafters.

15'-1½"

½" fibre board
ceiling

7'-5"

BATHROOM. HALL

2" screed

glazed
light

radtr.

4"x3" wood
post

LIVING ROOM

balustrade

COVERED WAY

3" diam.
post

GARAGE

½" composition floor
4" site concrete, 6" hardcore.

SECTION B-B. Scale: ⅛ in.=1 ft

The south side of the house at Dorking designed by Bevil Greenfield. The garage, a corner of which can be seen on the left, is connected to the main building by a covered way and the fuel store. The site slopes steeply southwards from the road and there are fine views of Leith Hill to the south-west and of Dorking town and Box Hill to the south-east.

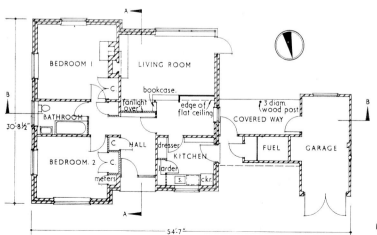

BEDROOM 1

LIVING ROOM

C

bookcase.

fanlight
over

edge of
flat ceiling

3" diam.
wood post

B

BATHROOM

30'-8½"

COVERED WAY

B

C

HALL

dresser

FUEL

GARAGE

BEDROOM. 2

C

KITCHEN

larder

meters

s.

ckr.

54'-7"

PLAN. Scale: ⅛ in.=1 ft

designed by **H. U. GERSON** (*architect*) **AND ALEXANDER GIBSON** (*assistant architect*)

The house from the north-east.

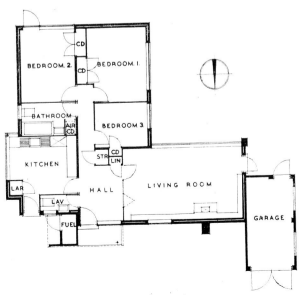

PLAN. Scale: $\frac{1}{16}$ in. = 1ft.

THE L-SHAPED PLAN was adopted to give:—
(1) ease for making possible future extensions,
(2) a sheltered sitting space, (3) exclusion from
the living room view of a house to the south-east.
(4) an informal atmosphere.

CONSTRUCTION. 10 in. cavity walls with $4\frac{1}{2}$ in.
brick outer skin and 3 in. hollow clay block inner
skin. $4\frac{1}{2}$ in. brick partitions to bedroom wing,
2 in. breeze elsewhere. *Roof:* 7 in. × 2 in. joists,
insulating board, $1\frac{1}{2}$ in. heavy duty woodwool
slabs and 3-ply felt with mineral dressing. *Floors:*
5 in. concrete finished with $\frac{5}{8}$ in. pine blocks laid
in bitumen. *Windows:* E.J.M.A. standard. *Garage:* walls of 6 in. concrete blocks with piers;
roof of woodwool slabs on standard r.c. farm-
roof units (licence prohibited bricks or timber).

HEATING. Slow combustion stove in living
room; electric points elsewhere. Hot-water
supply from 20 gallon electric water heater.

AREAS. 930 sq. ft, excluding garage. Living room
21 ft × 12 ft; bedroom 1 $12\frac{1}{2}$ ft × $10\frac{1}{2}$ ft; bedroom
2 $12\frac{1}{2}$ ft × $9\frac{1}{2}$ ft; bedroom 3 $9\frac{1}{4}$ ft × $7\frac{1}{2}$ ft.

COST. Approximately £1,200, excluding bedroom cupboards and various joinery fittings;
plus garage, £140. Approximately 25s. $9\frac{1}{2}$d. per
sq. ft, excluding garage.

Above: the south side of the living room. The joists and insulating board ceiling are left in their own natural colours. Left: the house from the south-west. Walls are faced with white sand-lime bricks and gutters and downpipes are of pressed steel. The house, built in 1947, is on a hilltop with a fine view to the south-west.

designed by **ARNE JACOBSEN**

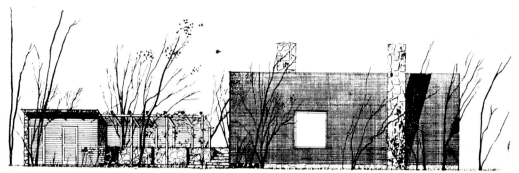

North elevation

THIS SUMMER HOUSE was built on the edge of the Kullen Downs in 1944 for two Danish doctors. It contains a living room, a kitchen and one bedroom, and on the east side there is a pergola leading to a garden shed and an outside water-closet adjoining it.

CONSTRUCTION. Walls of frame construction with painted boards outside and natural pine boards inside. Chimney, terrace, garden path and end wall of garden shed in local stone. *Roof:* shingle roof on triangular battens on hardboard. Ceiling in living room 2 in. × 1 in. planed strip boards; ceilings elsewhere in 1 in. insulight board. *Floors:* varnished pine wood flooring.

COST. 21.000 Danish crowns. Approximately £1,100 in 1944.

The living room.

The terrace and dining porch, which face west.

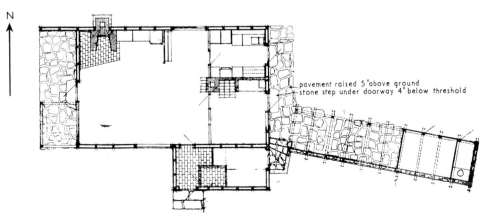

N

pavement raised 5" above ground
stone step under doorway 4" below threshold

PLAN. Scale: $\frac{1}{16}$ in. = 1 ft

designed by **ERIC LYONS**

The group of four houses for old people built at Weston Green, Esher, and designed by Eric Lyons, viewed from the south-west. The houses are planned with a minimum of circulation space, and there is a fuel store and another store easily accessible immediately outside the kitchen door. A feature of these houses is the bay windows and the large partly covered entrance porches.

THE HOUSES ILLUSTRATED here consist of a group of four single-storey houses for old people which were built as part of a housing scheme in Longmead Road, at Weston Green, Esher, for the Esher Urban District Council. The site of the housing scheme covers an area of over ten acres and the other buildings in the layout include two blocks of flats and groups of three and four-bedroom houses. One of the blocks of flats can be seen in the background, beyond the single-storey houses, in the illustration above. The old people's houses face towards the south, and they were completed in 1953.

CONSTRUCTION. 11 in. cavity load-bearing external walls and 4½ in. load-bearing brick partitions. Walls plastered internally. Walls of stores in 4½ in. rendered brickwork. *Roof:* reinforced concrete hollow block slabs, with foamed slag screed and ¾ in. asphalt. *Floors:* 5 in. concrete floor finished with ⅝ in. coloured mastic asphalt, and with quarry tiles in kitchen. *Ceilings:* plastered on underside of concrete slab. *Windows:* modified English Joinery Manufacturers' Association wood windows.

HEATING. Open fire in living room with Redfyre No. 4 back-boiler.

AREAS. Each house: 410 sq. ft, excluding porch. Living room 12 ft × 10 ft; bedroom 12¾ ft × 10 ft (including built-in cupboard); kitchen 8 ft × 7¾ ft.

COST. Contract price for four old people's bungalows: £4,500. Cost per sq. ft: 44s. Cost per ft cube: 3s. 6d.

PLAN. Scale: $\frac{1}{16}$ in. = 1 ft

A detail of the entrance to one of the old people's houses at Esher. Each house contains a living room, one bedroom 12 feet 9 inches long by 10 feet wide, a kitchen and a bathroom with w.c. The spacious porch shown in the illustration above is finished in asphalt on screed on a reinforced concrete slab, except where it is left uncovered. The fascia beam is also in reinforced concrete, and the porch is supported by 3 inch steel columns. The walls below the large bay window are finished externally with 6 inch by 6 inch coloured tiles.

designed by **IMRIE, PORTER AND WAKEFIELD**

THIS PAIR OF HOUSES for old people (designed by the late G. Blair Imrie, T. McEwan Porter and Peter Wakefield) are typical of several other one-storey houses built as part of this housing scheme. They face south, were built in 1950, and were designed in accordance with the *Housing Manual 1949* and to pass the Ministry of Health costing system. Construction and finishes were therefore kept as simple as possible for economy.

CONSTRUCTION. Concrete foundations. External cavity walls of Marston valley brick facings with wide buff-coloured mortar joints and 4 in. clinker block inner skin. Cavity party walls. *Roof:* Marley concrete pantiles on T.D.A. timber trusses; glass wool quilt over ceiling joists. *Floors:* solid floors finished with Marley tiles and wood blocks. *Windows:* S.M. casements in concrete frames. Walls and ceilings are distempered, the joinery painted, doors and stairs are finished with Stainex and bathroom has tiled splashes.

HEATING. Claco Midget Combination grate with back-boiler in living room. Cooking by electricity or gas.

AREAS. 662 sq. ft, plus 106 sq. ft for outbuilding. Living room 14 ft × 12 ft; bedroom 1 13 ft × 11 ft; bedroom 2 11 ft × 10 ft; kitchen 12 ft × 7 ft.

COST. Cost of 8 houses (as part of contract for 52 dwellings in all): £9,325. Cost of each house per sq. ft: 30s. 4¼d.

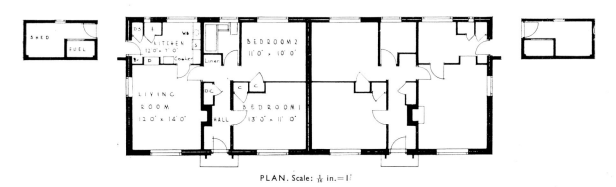

PLAN. Scale: 1/16 in. = 1'

APPENDIX

Floor panel heating

THE HEATING OF THE SMALL HOUSE is a problem to which both architects and house-owners are now giving ever-increasing attention—particularly now that many houses have an open-plan, where, as often as not, the hall leads into the living room without a doorway, and where the large living area may only be separated from the dining space by a removable screen.

It is not proposed to discuss here all the many systems of heating now adopted. The notes under the heading of *Heating*, appended to each text description of the houses illustrated on the previous pages give an indication of some of the methods used. It is proposed, however, to mention one particular system, namely floor panel heating. As this system is comparatively new to this country, it may be of interest to describe the installations in a few of the houses illustrated.

The principle of sub-floor heating is by no means an invention of our times, for the Romans had a similar arrangement in which steam or hot water warmed the floor from beneath; in fact, the only true difference between now and then lies in the application of present day methods of raising the heat and circulating it. For some considerable time floor heating has been employed in America, and it seems that the type most favoured there is heating by warm air.* In this country, on the other hand, it is only within the last few years that it has come into use.

The heating panels are embedded in the flooring material which extends throughout the house, and heat can be supplied to these panels in three main ways: by hot water, by warmed air or by electricity. In the case of hot water, the heating panels are coils of piping, either of iron or of copper, and the floor in which they are embedded should preferably be of concrete since this material is a poor conductor and retains the heat. The water is heated by a boiler and is then pumped through the panel circuits and back to the boiler again. With warmed air, it is unnecessary to instal pipes beneath the floor; instead, a series of ducts are constructed to run through the flooring materials. One method of constructing these is to form 'mouseholes' by inserting Ductubes† in the concrete floor when it is being laid. The air, heated by an electric battery, is circulated through these ducts. In floor-warming by electricity, circuits of resistance wire are embedded in the concrete floor and warmed by passing a current through them. A matter of importance is the insulation of walls, floors and ceilings. Insulation is necessary, in particular, at the edges around the external perimeter of the floor.

As regards the capital cost of installation, although this is fairly high, it is offset by low running costs. Thus, if a long-term view is taken, it may be seen that an initial expenditure which enables the whole house to be comfortably warmed through the winter can be counter-balanced by the low annual running costs.‡

The notes that follow describe the floor heating systems installed in three of the houses which are illustrated in this book. Two houses use hot water and one uses warmed air. In addition, there is a note concerning a house at Otham, designed by Brian Peake (which is not illustrated in this book), where the floor is warmed by circuits of electric wiring; and, finally, there is an example of floor heating in a house at Norwich where the hot water circulating in the floor panels is heated by means of a heat pump.§

Floor Panel Heating by Hot Water. (House at Gortnamoney, Northern Ireland, designed by E. W. Beaumont. Heating consultant: J. R. W. Murland. See pages 26 to 28 and page 108.)

The heating of this house is of especial interest in that care has been taken to deal by automatic means with almost every change in temperature that might occur, both inside and outside the house. Exceptional features are:

(*a*) a pilot control outside the house which over-

---

* Frank Lloyd Wright, both in his autobiography and in his book, *The Natural House* (published by Horizon Press Inc., pages 98–101), claims to have been the first architect to have introduced floor panel heating into America. He obtained the idea when in Japan, in 1914. Not until 1937, however, when he built the Jacobs House, was he able to put it into practice.

† Inflated rubber tubes, which are inserted in the concrete floor when it is being poured, and which are deflated and extracted after the floor has set, thus leaving ducts or 'mouseholes'.

‡ The cost of installation depends, of course, upon the size of the house and the complexity of the system put in. To give one specific case of a recent house of 1,050 square feet, the complete cost of installing the heating panels, the boiler, the mixing valves and all accessories, was £354. This installation is not automatic to the same extent as the one in the house in Northern Ireland, for which expense was not spared (see pages 108 and 109).

§ A series of articles on the subject of floor panel heating were published in *The Architects Journal*, February 19th, 1953.

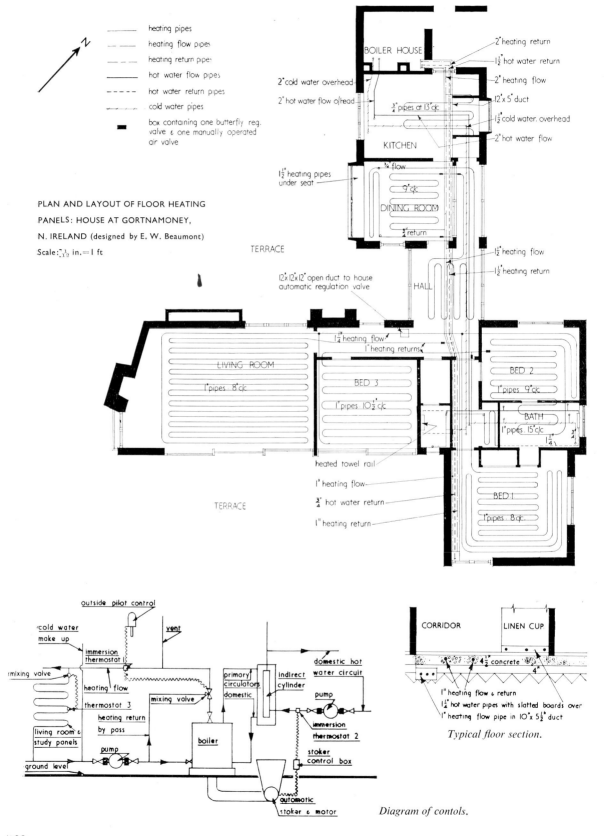

heating pipes
heating flow pipes
heating return pipes
hot water flow pipes
hot water return pipes
cold water pipes

box containing one butterfly reg. valve & one manually operated air valve

PLAN AND LAYOUT OF FLOOR HEATING
PANELS: HOUSE AT GORTNAMONEY,
N. IRELAND (designed by E. W. Beaumont)
Scale: $\frac{1}{12}$ in.=1 ft

BOILER HOUSE

2"cold water overhead
2" hot water flow o/head

KITCHEN

2"heating return
1½" hot water return
2" heating flow
12"x 5" duct
1½"cold water. overhead
2" hot water flow

1½" heating pipes under seat

¾" flow
9" c/c

DINING ROOM

¾" return

TERRACE

1½"heating flow
1½" heating return

HALL

12"x12"x12" open duct to house automatic regulation valve

1¼"heating flow
1" heating returns

LIVING ROOM
1" pipes 8" c/c

BED 3
1" pipes 10½" c/c

BED 2
1" pipes 9" c/c

BATH
1" pipes 15" c/c
¾"
1¼"

heated towel rail

TERRACE

1" heating flow
¾" hot water return
1" heating return

BED 1
1" pipes 8" c/c

outside pilot control

cold water make up

vent

immersion thermostat 1

mixing valve

heating flow thermostat 3

heating return

by pass

living room & study panels

ground level

pump

boiler

mixing valve

primary circulators

domestic

indirect cylinder

domestic hot water circuit

pump

immersion thermostat 2

stoker control box

automatic stoker & motor

Diagram of contols.

CORRIDOR   LINEN CUP.

4½" concrete
4"

1" heating flow & return
1¼" hot water pipes with slatted boards over
1" heating flow pipe in 10"x 5½" duct

Typical floor section.

108

rides the thermostat (inside the house) which regulates the amount of heat supplied to the floor panels. Thus, when the outside temperature rises, the pilot compels the thermostat to operate the heating at a lower temperature;

(b) a continuous-running pump with an automatic mixing valve controlled by a thermostat;

(c) separate control for living room and bedroom 3, which, since the double-glazed windows face south, get more heat from the sun than the other rooms;

(d) an automatically stoked boiler with the stoker controlled by the demand for hot water. Solid fuel is used.

Circuit and General Design. Hot water is taken from the boiler to an indirect cylinder for domestic hot water, and through a mixing valve and a continuous-running pump to the floor panels for heating purposes. The mixing valve is controlled by a regulator thermostat which automatically opens and closes this valve, thereby regulating (i) the amount of hot water from the boiler and (ii) the amount of water re-circulating through the bye-pass, to balance the heating input with the heat loss from the house. The regulator thermostat is electrically connected to an outside pilot which is responsive to the external factors which determine the heat loss from a building—temperature, wind, rain and sun. The pilot overrides the normal setting of the regulator thermostat and allows it to operate at a lower temperature when the outside temperature rises.

Boiler and Stoker. The boiler is fired by an automatic underfeed stoker, also controlled by a thermostat. Again, the water is circulated by an electric pump which is never switched off, and the stoker is automatically brought into action when the temperature of the water falls below that at which the thermostat is set. It is also brought into action for a pre-determined period during every hour by an overriding electrical timing device. This prevents the fire from going out when the heat loss from the house is so small that the thermostat would not bring the stoker into action.

The Panels. The heating panels laid under the concrete floor consist of black iron pipes $\frac{3}{4}$ inch or 1 inch in diameter, welded together and connected to the main flow and return pipes. They are laid at varying centres. To prevent some panels running cold, each circuit has a butterfly regulating valve under a small access panel in the floor, as well as an air vent to release air locks.

The panels are embedded in the 4-inch site concrete under which is a 4-inch layer of vermiculite concrete, except in the kitchen where the difficulty is to get rid of heat rather than to conserve it. Here the pipes are laid directly on hardcore. The panels in the living room and bedroom 3 have a separate thermostatic control, which is electrically connected to a motorized valve on the branch feeding these two panels. The object is to regulate separately the flow of heat to these two rooms which face south and have double-glazing and become much warmer than the other rooms. This thermostat is set at 65° F. There is also a fireplace in the living room, and the thermostatic control of the heating panels in this room regulates the temperature when the fire is alight, without causing any reduction of heat in other rooms.

The flow temperature immediately above the mixing valve varies from 110° to 150° F. according to the weather conditions, and the air temperature is kept fairly steadily between 60° and 65° F.

The Controls. In the coldest weather the stoker is left on the day position all night, but, when the outside temperature gets above 36° F., the night control is used for economy and, in this case, the general temperature drops below the comfort level but soon recovers in the morning. Except in very cold weather, the stoker control is set to cut out at 125° to 130° F.

Floor Panel Heating by Hot Water. (House at Chorley Wood, Herts, designed by C. B. Ratcliffe. See pages 39 to 41.)

A cast-iron boiler with a damper serves the low pressure warming system and heats the hot water storage calorifier. The boiler is in the kitchen and burns coke or anthracite. The temperature of the water is maintained at the degree necessary to heat the water in the calorifier, and the temperature of water feeding the warming system is reduced by a three-port electrically operated mixing valve. This valve is controlled by an immersion thermostat, adjusted according to the weather.

The floor throughout contains steel pipe coils embedded in the 4-inch thick concrete floor slab, the depth of embedding and spacing of the pipes being varied to suit the usage of the particular room. There are seven pipe circuits, each controlled by a double regulating valve. Round the perimeter of the floor there is insulation consisting of 1-inch compressed cork slabs stuck to the site slab with bitumen. A granolithic finish is used for the floor screeding.

The lounge and dining room have, in addition, pipe coils in one wall. Two bedrooms and part

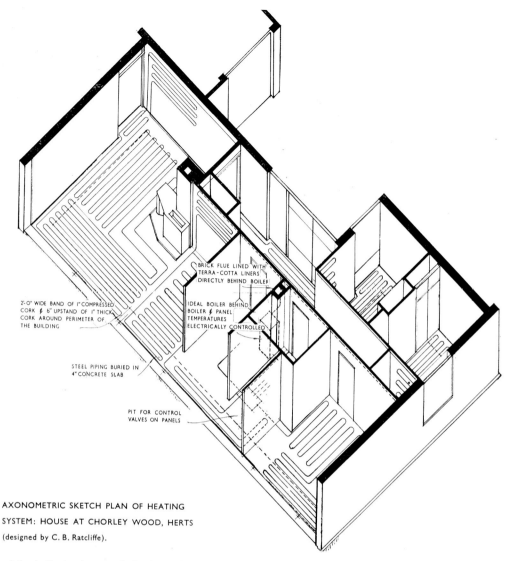

2'-0" WIDE BAND OF 1" COMPRESSED
CORK & 6" UPSTAND OF 1" THICK
CORK AROUND PERIMETER OF
THE BUILDING

BRICK FLUE LINED WITH
TERRA-COTTA LINERS
DIRECTLY BEHIND BOILER

IDEAL BOILER BEHIND.
BOILER & PANEL
TEMPERATURES
ELECTRICALLY CONTROLLED

STEEL PIPING BURIED IN
4" CONCRETE SLAB

PIT FOR CONTROL
VALVES ON PANELS

AXONOMETRIC SKETCH PLAN OF HEATING

SYSTEM: HOUSE AT CHORLEY WOOD, HERTS

(designed by C. B. Ratcliffe).

of the hall also have coils in the wall. These provide extra warmth for the children to do their homework in their own rooms and for the owner to work at his desk in one corner of the hall. The walls heated thus are either portions of the inner leaf of the cavity walls or portions of the internal partitions. They are constructed of breeze blocks, cork sheeting an inch thick, a layer of fine concrete (in which the coils are embedded) and have a finish of plaster. This plaster is of a special specification: a mixture of hydrated lime, pit sand, hair and plaster of paris. Normally a $\frac{1}{8}$-inch mesh canvas screen is incoporated at the surface of the setting coat, but this technique was varied and expanded metal mesh was applied (as for pipe coils in suspended ceilings).

The bathroom is planned next to the kitchen, so that the length of the primary pipes between the boiler and the hot water storage calorifier are to a minimum.

The water is circulated through the embedded pipes by an electrically driven centrifugal pump having change-over valves so that the flow of water can be reversed. It can flow either first through the wall coils and then through the floor coils or *vice-versa*. The installation has not been working a full winter's season but results to date are very satisfactory. It cost £650 to instal, and it is estimated that the running costs should work out at approximately five tons of broken coke per year (this includes heating the domestic hot water as well as the floor panels).

Floor Panel Heating by Warmed Air. (House at Caversham, near Reading, designed by Booth and Ledeboer. See page 8 to 51).

This heating system was designed by the owner, a heating engineer.* There is floor heating throughout (except in the dining room which has a hot water radiator), but warmed air is used instead of hot water. The air is circulated from a heating battery into a main-flow duct and then, *via* a series of smaller ducts or 'mouseholes' which run parallel to each other through the concrete floor, it passes to the return duct which leads back to the battery. The main flow and return ducts are 18 inches by 12 inches in size, while the 'mouseholes' are 3 inches in diameter and were formed in the concrete floor itself, when constructed, by means of Ductubes.† The distance between the 'mouseholes' varies according to the needs of the room.

The under-floor air is heated and circulated in the following way. Water, heated in a boiler fired by a Pillinger oil-firing unit, is pumped to, and warms, a Copperad heating battery. This battery warms the air, which is then blown through the ducts under the floor by a fan driven by a half h.p. motor. (This motor also drives the pump which circulates the water from the boiler to the heating battery.) The boiler serves the dining room radiator and the domestic hot water calorifier.

Automatic control is effected by: (*a*) a water thermostat to start and stop the Pillinger oil-firing unit; (*b*) a Teddington thermal valve in the return pipe from the Copperad battery, which is responsive to the air returning from the under-floor ducts; (*c*) a Venner clock switch which runs the fan morning and evening a length of time pre-set according to season; (*d*) a room thermostat which cuts out the clock switch if the house is warm enough to need no supplementary heating. These controls maintain temperatures constant within 2° or 3° F. in all weathers.

The air is circulated under the floor on closed-circuit, and is not released into the rooms. Grills were provided to admit warmed air to the rooms, but these are kept closed as the sense of comfort with floor heating alone has proved better. With this sub-floor heating, in the opinion of the owner, there is a greater feeling of warmth without stuffiness than with a hot water radiator system or other systems. The floor need only be about

7° above room temperature, and the latter can be some 5° lower than with a radiator heating system.

A check of the running cost showed that the oil consumption was about 3.9 gallons per day. At 1s. 3d. per gallon the whole house and all domestic hot water can thus be heated for about 34s. per week.

Floor Panel Heating by Electricity. (House at Otham, Kent, designed by Brian Peake.)

In a recent article, the architect has described the method of floor warming this house by means of electricity.‡ The installation consists of two separate circuits of resistance wire embedded in a 2 inch thickness of screed on top of 5 inches of concrete and 4 inches of hardcore. One circuit serves the living room (an area of approximately 530 square feet) with a loading of 5 kW. The other circuit serves the main bedroom, the dressing room, the entrance hall and the lobby (a total area of approximately 470 square feet) with a loading of 3kW. Each circuit is controlled by two thermostats, one air-thermostat being situated in a strategic position on the wall of one of the rooms in question, and the other has its head buried in the thickness of the concrete floor to control the temperature to which the slab is allowed to rise.

Mr. Peake gives the following reasons why he chose electricity as the heat source:
1. Absolutely no attention required and no stoking, cleaning, etc.
2. No deterioration to pipes or water flooding.
3. No space required for boiler, fuel store, etc.
4. No floor space lost to radiators, etc.
5. Absolute cleanliness in operation.
6. Lower cost of installation.

The total cost of installation (including two towel airers placed in the bathroom) was £287 11s. 8d. The running cost for one year, including (beside the floor heating) all cooking, refrigeration, lighting and water heating was £127 12s. 3d. It must be taken into account here that it was not possible to obtain from the local supply company a cheap rate for heating only, or a reduced night rate. Furthermore, this running cost figure covered the first year after the heating was installed, and it is estimated that twenty to thirty per cent of the heating can be lost in the first year in drying out a

---

* Mr. Colin Allsebrook, A.M.I.Mech.E., to whom thanks are due for permission to publish the above note. A description of this installation appeared in *The Industrial Heating Engineer* (London), November, 1954 and also in *Architectural Design*, November, 1953.

† See footnote on page 107.

‡ This house was illustrated in *The Architect and Building News*, April 29th, 1954. The note above is based on Mr. Peake's article in that number. The area of the house is 1,500 square feet.

Another article on electrical floor warming in general was published in an earlier issue, April 22nd, 1954.

new house. Ensuing years should, therefore, show an improved performance.

The life of the embedded wire is not accurately known, although the manufacturers are optimistic about this. Should renewal be necessary, the screeded surface would have to be hacked up.

Floor Panel Heating by Hot Water heated by a Heat Pump. (Plant and installation designed by John A. Sumner.)

This experimental plant was installed in a house built for Mr. Sumner in 1950. The floor area is approximately 1,600 square feet and the accommodation consists of a hall, sitting and dining rooms, kitchen, two bedrooms and a bathroom. The rising cost of coal led to the investigation into the use of the heat pump, powered by an electric motor, as an alternative to the solid fuel, gas or oil-fired boiler.

One of the functions of the heat pump can be to raise low-grade low temperature heat to a commercially useful temperature and, by means of heat exchangers, to make this available for space-heating purposes. Low-grade heat can be extracted from water (e.g. from a lake, river, well or even the sea), from the atmosphere or the soil. Very briefly, the water is drawn from its source by a circulating water pump and passes through a pipe coil within an evaporator (cooler) containing a refrigerant, such as freon, which is capable of changing from a liquid to gaseous state at temperatures that are available in the low-grade heat source. This gaseous refrigerant is then drawn into the compressor where it is compressed to a pressure corresponding to the useful temperature required (i.e. 80° to 140° F.) It is then transferred to the second heat exchanger, the condenser (heater). Since the medium to be heated, for space heating purposes, is at a lower temperature than the high temperature gaseous refrigerant, the latter gives up to it its latent heat and is thereby condensed. The refrigerant then passes through an expansion valve and the process is repeated.

In this installation at Norwich, the low-grade heat source is from the soil, and the rooms are heated by hot water circulating in 800 feet of copper tube laid in the concrete sub-floor. This tubing is divided into eight coils each with a control valve. The system is designed such that between October and April the air temperature, day and night, never falls below 60° F. nor rises above 65° F. Local control is by means of two thermostats, and the variation in temperature throughout the house never exceeds 1° F.

Before the heat pump was installed, tests were carried out to obtain a steady, measured source of heat. For this purpose an immersion heater loaded to 8.4 kW. was used. Comparing these results with those of the heat pump, it was found that the heat pump involved a maximum expenditure of electrical energy of 3.6 kW. (which included the ground coil circulating pump), whilst a 10.1 kW. electric immersion heater would be required to achieve the same conditions. Taking fuel and electricity prices in Norfolk as a basis, comparative seasonal costs were as follows (assuming a constant temperature of 60° F.):

Heat pump	£36
Coal or coke	£59
'Raw' electricity	£89

The advantages of economic running costs and the absence of solid fuel, with its dust, cleaning and constant attention, assures a future for this type of heating unit, which is completely automatic. Production in quantity of two types of heat pump using air as the low-grade heat source is predicted for 1956. One type will heat air which can be passed through ducts to warm rooms, whilst the other will produce warmed water to pass through pipe coils in the floor or ceiling. Although the cost may exceed that of the conventional installation, it is expected that this additional expenditure will be met by the annual savings in running costs over the first five or six years.

ABBREVIATIONS

(The following abbreviations have been used in the text notes to the houses illustrated between pages 16 to 106.)

D.P.C.:	damp-proof course
E.J.M.A.:	English Joinery Manufacturers' Association
r.c.:	reinforced concrete
R.S.J's:	rolled steel joists
S.M.:	standard metal (windows)
t. and g.:	tongued and grooved
T.D.A.:	Timber Development Association.